NO GREAT STORY STARTED WITH A SALAD

MENJA BÉ, CAGA FORT I NO TINGUIS POR A LA MORT

Eat well, shit hard and don't be afraid of death.
Old Catalan toast

All enquires to: oli@olimax,com
www.olimax.com

Extreme Lunching

OLIMAX

OLIMAX

I've worked in photography and design since the early 1980's.
My portraits have been featured in such publications as The Face, ID, Time Out, Actuel, Libération, American Harpers, The British Journal of Photography, The Sunday Times and The Guardian to name a few.

My interactive digital media work includes the multimedia site for Primal Scream's XTRMNTR, featured in the Museum for Applied Arts in Frankfurt, an innovative artificial intelligence application for Simple Kid, which won the BT Interactive Music Award 2003 and digital projects for Amnesty International & The Institute of Contemporary Arts among many others.

After buggering about with music technology for a few years, remarkably I signed a record contract with Warner Brothers on my thirty three and a third birthday. At the time I jokingly said I would not continue past 45. That birthday was my last day in a studio.

Arrogantly believing I was now in the entertainment industry and burdened with a room stacked full of over a decade's worth of negatives and transparency sheets, including the night-life I had been covering for Time Out and all my studio portraits, I casually tossed the bloody lot in a handy skip. I was to regret that no more than when the V&A asked me to use them for a show.

In the recording studio I have produced and mixed albums for such diverse artists as Mick Jones & Big Audio Dynamite, Mark E. Smith's The Fall, The Grid and The Tiger Lillies, including a soundtrack for the musical Shock Headed Peter, which won two Olivier Awards in 2002. Big Audio Dynamite's Rush/Change of Atmosphere was honoured with Billboard Magazine's Rock Single of the Year and was number one in many territories. I am still waiting to get paid!

Since then, returning to formal studio photography after a long hiatus, I worked on, for want of a better term, mass portrait events. Finding a location, perhaps a gallery, club or pub, I set up a makeshift studio. Participants are asked to bring an object relevant to the theme. The intention is to invoke a party atmosphere. I usually try to shoot about a hundred portraits over the course of the day. Fortunately I have a wonderful team. The ensuing portraits from each event have formed the basis for a subsequent book and exhibition.

For the last 15 odd years I have resided in Catalonia for reasons of cultural health.

In 2019 I opened Gros, a bar and restaurant in Calella, Catalonia, just prior to the COVID pandemic decimating the world and destroying the hospitality industry. Not great timing.
After four years I just got out alive, although a whole lot poorer for it.

In between all this malarkey I have travelled the world in search of the bizarre, the offbeat and the plain disgusting to salivate the palate. It is a sickness of sorts but curiosity and greed prevail.

This book is intended as a testament to those times.

Design: olimax.com
Photography: olipix.com
Music: olimix.com

School's Out

I grew up in a household that was very much focused around the kitchen. From an early age, on Saturday afternoon I might be helping my Pa pull the bones out from a boiled pig's head to make brawn or dress a whole salmon with cucumber scales.

My parents were very adventurous in culinary skill and knowledge at a time when garlic was considered evil foreign muck. The only place that sold olive oil was the chemist. They went to 'continental cookery' classes every week, returning, rather refreshed, clutching, maybe, a Barbary duck that they had just learnt to bone out whole and stuff, or a cassoulet, ready to cook in the stove for many hours, in a Le Creuset Dutch oven, bought for the purpose.

Friday nights there was often a cocktail party where I was bidden to pass around the hors d'oeuvres and later serve the drinks. Once I had been sent to bed I would creep halfway down the stairs to listen in on the conversations, not that I understood much once the booze had kicked in (the guests', not mine). These were noisy hedonistic affairs though no car keys on the table, at least as far as I noticed. Shame in a way as all the guests drove home afterwards though the country night. No breathalyser then and no socially responsible drinking advice from the authorities.

Saturday nights were for dinner parties and this is where the folks recently acquired skills were presented to the assembly although some of the guests would bring a course. One of his favourites was pa's CEO, Dean, an American. His wife was from the mid west and her contribution was, for the most part, some bizarre creation always involving something in aspic, chicken and sweetcorn in orange jelly for example. Dig out old 1950s cooking pamphlets if you have never seen these monstrous creations though I have always fancied doing a dinner entirely of these without warning the guests.

Of course there was a collection of recipe books in the house, not just anywhere but in the downstairs loo and this is where the real research took place, roughly working on the principal of one in, one out, that is, a recipe for each sitting. My poor Pa overran this once to his dismay. He used to smoke on the bog and, while deeply engrossed in a recipe, the end of his fag dropped off and landed in his pants, instantly setting fire to his trousers around his ankles, a most tricky dilemma. I am not sure how he resolved to get out with both his dignity and wedding tackle intact but, to his credit, he put in an insurance claim for the cost of a new 3-piece bespoke suit, as was the one he had torched the pants of. Remarkably the claim was paid without question. I feel that it was such a ridiculous story that the underwriters, once they had stopped pissing themselves laughing, had to believe it.

Since then I have been obsessed with collecting cook books, though less relevant now with the internet, your own personal library. Pre-web it was such joy to flick through various tomes, both ancient and modern, to discover new ideas for dinner, to then go out in search of obscure ingredients, spices and tools from all through the specialist shops spread across London and beyond. Amazon just does not have the same thrill.

I have had several collections of books, each time disposing of then only to start again, the greatest one reaching 992 in number just before I decanted myself to Spain, where, once again, I began over, only this time, apart from a few classics, they were Spanish or Catalan. My language skills are desperately inadequate but I can read a restaurant menu of the most obscure ingredients better than some natives. La Carta spoken here.

Bon profit.

Stove-side Reading

MASTERING THE ART OF FRENCH COOKING
Simone Beck and Julia Child 1961
This is my desert island cookbook. Originally written for the U.S. market it was rejected by the first publisher as being too complicated for Americans. It is the definitive guide to classic French cuisine. For 30 years or more I had an increasingly tatty copy that eventually fell apart from daily use. A joy to read, one cannot help hearing Julia Child's Muppet-like voice. Follow the recipes precisely and you too will soon master the art of French cooking.

THE GENTLEMAN'S COMPANION
or Around the World with Jigger, Beaker and Flask - Charles H. Baker, Jr. 1939
In 1926, to escape prohibition, Baker joined a world cruise as PR officer, where he met his heiress wife. For the next quarter of a century they sailed the planet in search of exotic drink and drinking companions, among them Ernest Hemingway, William Faulkner, Douglas Fairbanks and Errol Flynn which he wrote about in Esquire,and Gourmet and formed the backbone of his two volume set, The Gentleman's Companion. Like Waterhouse on lunch, it is not so much about the recipes, of which a lot are given, but about the experience of drinking.

THE THEORY AND PRACTICE OF LUNCH
Keith Waterhouse 1986
If there is one book that could be called the bible of lunching it is this. As he makes very clear from the start, this is not about food but of lunch, its ways, its rules and its purpose. I must have given away about 50 copies by now. Long out of print, if you're outbid on Ebay, it's me.

THE FOOD LAB: Better Home Cooking Through Science
Kenji López-Alt 2015
Kenji heads the essential web site, Serious Eats. He finds the best way to cook anything through thorough experimentation, trying temperatures, timings and additives, until he has the definitive combination so you

don't have to.

ON FOOD AND COOKING
Harold McGee 2004
The science of cooking in a readable form for even the most illiterate chef. Once you can understand what is going on in the pan cooking becomes second nature.

NOSE TO TAIL EATING - A Kind of British Cooking
Fergus Henderson 1998
There is little doubt that at the end of the last century Fergus single handedly changed the face of British dining for ever, bringing our own heritage to the fore where once it had held its head in shame in deference to Italian, French, Indian and the like. This straight forward tome is the bible of simple British fare. As the title suggests the philosophy involves every part of the animal. Not for the faint-hearted and certainty not for vegetarians, it is offaly good.

ENGLISH SEAFOOD COOKERY
Rick Stein 1988
Well you have to have one seafood book and this is it. Containing no photos, though some illustrations, Stein's first book, published before he became well known, makes for great reading.

DICKTALES or 'Thankyous and Sluggings'
Dick Bradsell 2022
This is not, as you may imagine from the maestro, a book of cocktails. It may contain many but it is about, and written by, Dick. Illustrated by clippings, letters, doodles and old photos it is a scrapbook covering the journey of his life, by the way of drinks, dives, dresses and D & D.

FLOYD'S FOOD
Keith Floyd 1981
Any of his book will do though his first is a good start. It's not the recipes, it is the presence of the old soak lurking behind them. Have a quick flick through, grab a bottle, take a 'quick slurp' and watch car crash TV but underneath a fond tribute to a legend in his own lunchtime.

The best advice given to me was by a friend, Jazz, who owns several restaurants and bars in Barcelona. He said do not attempt any decoration or refitting, do not spend money, until the establishment is up and running. Just open it up as soon as the lease is signed and start trading. Stubbornly and to my great cost I completely ignored it. I spent 9 months completely redesigning and redecorating the place, to great effect I have to say, but at great expense too. I wanted to make my mark.

Additionally it hadn't occurred to me that, surprisingly, I had a job. Although I spend all my free time in front of a computer or camera doing my other work, I haven't had to regularly go to a place of employment since my twenties and now I was obliged to. That was a shock. What a dick!

Gros finally opened for Easter 2019 and did pretty well considering. George joined us in July and he was a godsend. A native speaker of both Castilian and Catalan and a maestro of the cocktail he charmed the locals. We were doing pretty well. By the time we shut for the winter season in November the place was breaking-even, unprecedented for a new restaurant,

However 2020 didn't start well. The day before New Year's Eve I had a heart problem and spent the next three weeks in intensive care before being cut open. It was a foreboding of the year to come. At the beginning of March 2020 we restocked the bar, got fresh barrels of beer in, cleaned the place, top to bottom and did as much food prep as we could. I flew to London for a spot of extreme lunching, returning full of enthusiasm for the reopening. We lasted two days before the lockdown struck.

Peter Clark

I have to say I had a great lockdown. I had a huge house facing the sea and spent most of the time reading at the rate of a book a day while looking over George's shoulders watching food and drink documentaries. In the evening we took turns in the kitchen, using the food I had prepared for the opening, then strolled down to the restaurant to, ahem, 'clean the bar'.

When all drinking establishments were compulsorily shut there was one place that was open to the few, the best reason I ever found for owing a bar. We had restocked the draft beer for the opening so, genuinely, it would have gone off. Duty had to be done. After a while I had to phone the suppliers and order another couple of barrels. They questioned why we would need them when we were technically shut but were greatly amused and swiftly came through with the goods. Probably the first orders they had had for months.

Finally we reopened in June 2020 but the writing was on the wall. The locals, including our most loyal clients, still had the fear and were too used to fending for themselves at home. Gone were the tourists too. Although I had avoided the notion of a pub it has to be said that, in terms of the bar trade, the Catalans have no drinking culture, especially in suburban Calella where there appears to be no single people over 20. Whereas the British embrace irresponsible drinking heartily and have a wonderful disregard for official guidelines, much to the benefit of this landlord.

In the end I had to bottle out and cut my losses to great chagrin. When I first mooted this adventure I was wisely advised by friends not to go there. My chum Cadman, said "it would be like giving a machine gun to a monkey". Sound words but it had to be done. Would it be still there without the plague? Who knows but I gave it my best and I'd give it another go with what I have learnt under my belt and with your money.
Bon Profit, as we say here.

@ G R O S V E R M U T E R I A

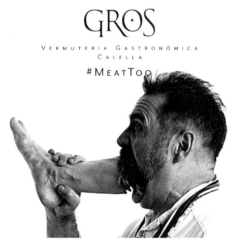

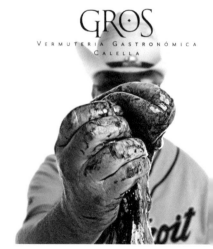

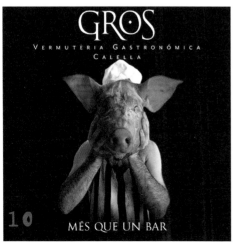

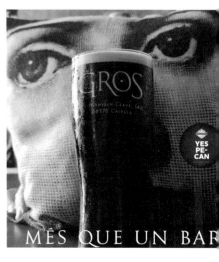

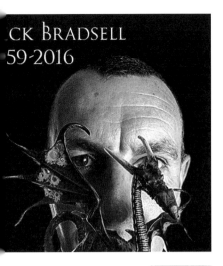

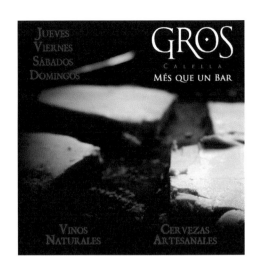

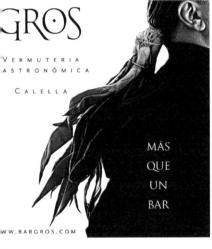

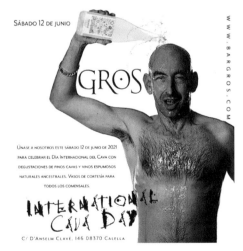

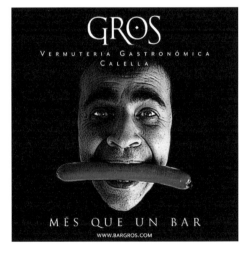

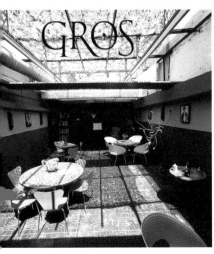

adams add adobo alchemy alter anderson appliance appreciate art ate au author bac

boil bone book bourdain bourguignon box braai

blanquette bleu boeuf

butchering butter buy cacciatora cacciatore cake camping canning capta

se chef chicken chill chisel chop res cla clean co

cookie cookline cookmaid cooko kpot co cook okstove co

culinary curry cutting dancing date de d dec

electricity en entertain esc en etna extractor fak fa f

reezing french fresh fricassee rittata fr

grill grillmaster grillroom g

gredient integrity iron irori ja

onnaise machine making manipulate marina

srepresent mix mixture modify molasses money

parboil parch parfry pasta pastry pastrycook

epare preserve pressu

roast roaster rosemar

risotto

e showering shrimp simmer skil

storing stove stov taking

12

ne unhung utensi

gar wangle w

ake baker balti banchan barbecue barbeque basin baste bbq be

read breakfast brewing brick bringing brisket broasted brochette broil broth br

amelise caramelize casserole catering celebrity change charcoal char

cook cookable cookbook coo

okware cool don cornbread counte craft create creative crisp cri

iet din nner dire sh di dress drinking dry du

fish fl etching florentine flour follow fondue

ly ger ginger going gourmet graham

ase household housekeeping housewo

tard lasagna laundry learning leaves lemon life li

s meatloaf medium merritt micro-cook micr

onions ordering orzo oven overboil overcook

enta polony pot potato potpie poussin prebal

ead ready recipe recoct refrigerate re

ing serve setting sewing sharing sheet

steak steam stew stic

toss trained travel turn unbaked un

workman zap

13

A WORD ABOUT SOUS VIDE

Reading through these recipes I realise how much I sometimes rely on it. For those that don't know, it is a method of vacuum sealing food and placing it in a water bath at an exact regulated, though modest, temperature for, often as not, a very long time. Days can pass until your dinner is done.

The advantage is that you can cook your meat accurately to a precise and even degree. If you like your steaks medium rare then medium rare it will be. Every bit of it, right the way through. No graduation from edge to centre. Just beautifully tender juicy pink meat.

Time in the bath is less important. For our steaks we would do between 1 to 3 hours perhaps but they could remain longer. The time taken, once the meat is at the required level will just affect the tenderness of it. Unfortunately this can lead to mushy meat in some restaurants, when the steaks have just been left in the bath all day. Just ask Giles Coren.

Once the province of only professional kitchens, it is now available to all and sundry. The two bits of kit required are a vacuum sealer and an immersion circulator (aka Sous Vide wand) , You can spend a lot on each of these but my advice would be to get the cheapest possible and bin them when they fail.

You will need a container for your bath. A large pot will do but those transparent packing cases are ideal. You get them in a variety of sizes. It's great to see a dozen steaks bobbing round in bags. To save on running costs keep a lid on through which you have cut a hole for the wand to fit in. Maybe wrap bubble-wrap around the sides. Even better float enough ping-pong balls to cover the whole surface of the water.

What you won't see is any browning on the outside, that delightful sweetness in meat caused by the Maillard reaction when amino acids and sugars collide under high temperature. You therefore must flash your steak quickly, just before serving, on a very hot pan to achieve that without changing the perfect colour inside.

A great advantage, and one that appeals to home and professional kitchens alike, is that, once cooked, having reached the minimum food-safe temperature the meat is pasteurised and can be kept in the fridge or freezer for possibly weeks. Just bring back up to an internal temperature of at least 54.4°C. This means that you could, for instance, cook 2 or 3 kg of belly pork, individually portioned, and you would have instant ready-meals for weeks.

Smokin'

When it comes to home smoking there are two types, cold and hot. We concern ourselves with the later. Cold smoking is a more elaborate process and tends to be done on a large scale. It is designed to impart flavour into the food but not actually cook it whereas, as you may guess, hot smoking cooks, flavours and tenderises all in one go.

Easiest but most costly way is with an electric cabinet smoker, such as a Bradley. These cost about 600 euros upwards and use dedicated wood chip 'bisquettes' They are the size of a mini-bar and need a good air outlet.

A cheaper option is an outdoor charcoal barbecue, many of which nowadays already come with a built in or bolt-on smoker function though if not you can wing it with a tray of wood chip on the coals if it has a lid.

Failing that it is quite possible to do it in a wok with a lid on a gas hob though your kitchen smoke alarm may kick off. In fact if it doesn't you may need to change the battery. Find a round mesh tray with legs or that fits the wok half way up, often supplied. Line the dry wok with tin foil and spread around either a load of wood-chip or, as with many Chinese dishes, a mix of sugar, rice and black tea. Stick the wok on a high flame with a very tight lid. As soon as the smoke turns a dark yellow turn the gas right down but still smoking. Give it 30 minutes and see how it looks.

My preferred home kit is an old fashioned Brooks Home Smoker, popular with fishermen who wish to smoke their catch fresh from the lake. Inside the metal box you scatter wood chips on the bottom, rest your food on a rack, stick the lid on and light some methylated spirit in a small dish underneath. Burning slowly with that characteristic blue flame, the meths lasts about 20/30 minutes. Once out leave for another 10/15 and you should be done. Works wonders with mackerel. Chicken or duck breasts might need a second round. You can always stick the meat in a sous vide to tenderise it first.

I have no idea how old the Brooks are, my guess would be late last century, but they often turn up on ebay. The last one I got was about 20 quid, unused, complete with sawdust and recipe book

GET YOUR KIT ON

MADAGASCAN WILD BLACK PEPPER (aka Voatsiperifery pepper)
Once you have discovered this deeply aromatic spice, there is no going back. One sniff of that heady fragrance and you're hooked. You will question the popularity of standard black peppercorns over these beauties. I suppose the cost could be a factor but that never held back the ubiquity of cocaine among chefs in the 80s. That and the fact that they clog up your standard pepper grinders. The answer to that problem lies below.

THE MICROPLANE SPICE MILL
I guess we all must have one or two Microplane graters. How can you not? But you will certainly need one of these for your newly acquired kilo of Voatsiperifery pepper. Now I have to tell that you will need a second for the Tonka Beans that you are about to discover. Accept no substitute. An essential bit of kit.

TONKA BEANS
... for which you will need a second Microplane spice grinder to save your finger tips when desperately rubbing the last of your beans on a sharp grater. The aroma might bring to mind vanilla, cinnamon, almonds, nutmeg but tonka is of a different class altogether. It brings a warm glow to both sweet and savoury dishes and raises cream based cocktails to a higher plane.
The seeds of the Cumaru tree, the beans contain a low level of natural coumarin, used in both the commercial food industry and in perfume houses. It is also found in lavender, licorice, strawberries and cherries. Unfortunately, due to some slight evidence showing ill effects from massive doses, the FDA have chosen to ban Tonka in the USA, leading to an odd black market amongst the leading chefs of New York and beyond. Some arrests have been made. Luckily I source mine from Germany. It's good gear, man!

THE BITTER TRUTH CUCUMBER BITTERS
For G&T drinkers this is a game changer. It heightens even the lowliest gin to new levels. Even Larious and Schweppes, the most popular combination of lesser Spanish bars. I often carry a bottle in my man bag.

It is important though to use a microdose dose, two or three drops being quite sufficient. The one exception I make is to my blend of choice, Nordés Galician Gin with Fever Tree Mediterranean Tonic, it's just too perfect to muck around with.

Blow Torch

One of the important chemical processes that occurs in cooking is the Maillard reaction, a reaction between amino acids and reducing sugars when heated. But enough with the science already. All that you need to know is that when you brown certain foods they get much tastier. Seared meats, fried onions, roast coffee, crunchy roast potatoes, the sweet crisp lid atop Crema Catalana, all would not be the same without it. At higher temperatures still you get caramelisation to boot. Who wants a steak, however rare, without a dark sweet crust. I've never understood the appeal of a bland Mozzarella unless grilled until it bubbles with golden joy.

This is where the blow torch can come in handy. Instant flame at your finger tips, it is an essential part of every kitchen. Not those sad little ones they sell in posh kitchen stores. Keep one for sparking up a spliff over the stove without taking your eyebrows off by all means. No, we are talking a serious industrial tool. Take yourself down to the nearest professional hardware store, the sort of place you'd be served by a chap in a brown coat. Look for the dented vans outside. Tell them that you need a hand held propane torch to melt copper tubing. They'll sort you out.

It'll come in handy when you want to take the hair off a pig's head and in seconds you can light a charcoal barbecue in a raging storm. Cheese on toast will never be the same again.
No wonder the richest man on earth started making flame throwers.
Just watch your fingers.

Knives

Many chefs take great pride in their leather roll of very expensive knives. A good knife is a thing of beauty, not just a tool but carries with it an aesthetic quality beyond functionality. I have Japanese knives, German knives and even American knives. They are a pleasure to hold and each cost me a great deal, yet mostly remain stuck to the magnetic bar next to the extractor.

My daily go to is a Victorinox Fibrox 18 cm butcher's knife with a yellow handle, about 20 quid to you. It does a great job. The trick with any knife is to constantly sharpen it on a diamond block, a quick swipe each time you use it. Beyond that I have a couple of Victorinox paring knives and a large mighty Chinese chopper.
That about covers it in my book.

COOKING CHOPSTICKS

Not those twigs you get in your local Chinese. These are long, really long. Don't fit diagonally across this book long. They won't even fit in your kitchen drawer but you don't want them to because you need them to hand. These will replace your nasty metal tongs. They will replace your whisk. You will be smashing up your scrambled egg before you're had your morning coffee. Bloody sight easier to clean than a wire whisk too. And when you break your wrist and are in plaster they are the only thing that can reach that bloody itch and give it a good scratch. Shoulder blades too.

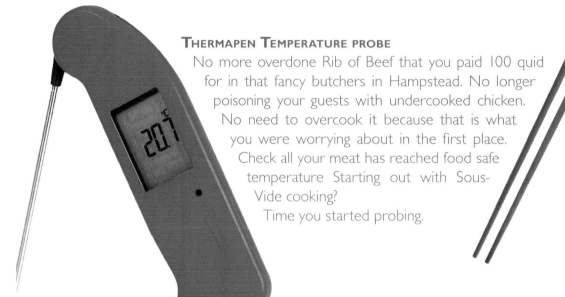

THERMAPEN TEMPERATURE PROBE

No more overdone Rib of Beef that you paid 100 quid for in that fancy butchers in Hampstead. No longer poisoning your guests with undercooked chicken. No need to overcook it because that is what you were worrying about in the first place. Check all your meat has reached food safe temperature Starting out with Sous-Vide cooking?
Time you started probing.

SILICONE WOK SPATULA

You're not still using wooden spoons are you? This is all you will need.
It is an extension of your right arm.
Not a little plastic thing to lick the cake mix out with. 35 cm tall, 10 cm wide at the business end with a wooden handle.
It even doubles as a food safe spanking paddle if you're in the mood.

POTATO RICER

Hopefully you have never tried mashing potatoes in a blender but even bashing with a potato masher is no fun. The late Joël Robuchon, international 3* Michelin chef with a huge restaurant chain defined his cuisine around mash, the crucial element being 50% butter. Wonderful but you have to start with perfect creamed spuds, Unless you want to break you wrist with a spud basher you need a ricer, the only way to get soft fluffy mash without the starch and proteins breaking up and letting your mash turn to wallpaper paste,
A ricer is the potato's friend.

ELECTRIC RICE COOKER

Sure you can cook rice in a saucepan with bits of tin foil and a lid but is it perfect every time? Since their invention in Japan in the 50s their prevalence has extended across the whole of Asia where now no household would be seen without at least one. Don't you think they might know all about rice?

Don't bother with those fancy European designer models. Get down to your local Asian grocery store and get the cheapest one they have but get a large one. When it stops working get another one immediately because by then you won't do without it. Just ask Uncle Roger. Fuiyoh

ICE CREAM MACHINE

A bit of an extravagance you may think but once you start you'll be trying new flavours every week and your guests will be so impressed they might think you can cook after all. Beetroot sorbet? Toast and Marmalade ice cream? Maple syrup and bacon ice cream? Pilchard sorbet? Well maybe not.

If you can afford it get one with a built in compressor like a Cuisinart but otherwise one of those Kenwood jobs for 30 quid where you pre-freeze the bucket does the trick.

LE CREUSET

If you can't wait until your parents are too week and feeble to steal theirs you may just have to buy your own. It doesn't last a lifetime, it lasts several if you look after it even with daily use and you will use it most days. Get a cast iron frying pan too and you don't need much more. Hideously expensive you can occasionally find them in markets but make sure the lining is intact or it is on the way out.

However if you can't run to the real thing, Lidl make a fairly decent fake for a quarter of the price. Do make sure it's orange though. Accept no less.

WHETSTONE

Throw away your knife steel. It never works. This is the only way to really get a decent sharp edge on your knives. Pop down the iron mongers and ask for a combination diamond sharpening block. Start sharpening on the course side. From the heal of the knife, with the blade at about 15 degrees to the stone, push forward down the length of the block sliding across to end up at the tip. Repeat towards you for the other side of the knife, always blade forward. When you have a decent edge flip the block over to finish on the fine side. Test it on a tomato.
If you want to get fancy get an India block but these need oil and it can get real messy.

19

On Baked Fish

Why do so many folk consider cooking fish difficult. Have they tried? Most fish are so wonderful you don't need to muck them about. All but the most delicate can be cooked in the oven with little effort.

Get an entire fish, cleaned and gutted but kept whole including its head and tail. Maybe sea bass, sea bream, turbot, brill, hake, tilapia, halibut, cod, grouper, haddock, catfish or snapper.

Preheat the oven to 200°C.

Rinse the fish under cold water and pat dry with paper towels. If you fancy, stuff whatever you have to hand inside it. A lemon slice, tarragon, coriander, cumin seeds, fresh fennel or fennel seeds, wild garlic, spring onions, fresh ginger or a slug of Pernod will all give extra depth to the flavour.

Oil the outside with kitchen roll, wiping along the fish from head to tail then sprinkle with coarse salt. Place in an oven dish and put it in the hot oven for about 20 minutes. It is done when you can push the flesh away from the backbone with little effort.

Remove from the oven. See. Cooking fish is easy.

On Poached Fish

Quite often the worse place to eat fish is by the sea. People who catch it are not necessarily the best at cooking, just as gynaecologists are not necessarily the best lovers.
A. A. Gill

Some fish fares much better poached in stock or, occasionally, milk. Salmon, trout and char, for example.
If you have a large fish then it is best to use a fish kettle. If small fillets then use a wide heavy bottomed pan.

Wash your fish then place it in the pan and almost cover with cold stock so there is just a bit of fish protruding.
Put on the hob at a low to medium heat and put the lid on.
If using a fish kettle you may need to put it across two rings.

Watch carefully, or just listen until you have a rolling bubble. Immediately turn the gas off and lift it away it from the heat, keeping the lid on tightly. Let it stand for 10/15 minutes, depending on the size.

For most of these fish, especially salmon, you want it slightly pink inside but the meat should still easily slide away from the bone. Use a couple of fish slices to lift it from the liquid on to a serving dish, removing the spine and bones in one piece which will easily pull away. If serving cold later, let it cool then put in the fridge or a cold larder if it is too big.

Of Haggis and Black Pudding

Fair fa' your honest, sonsie face, Great chieftain o the puddin'-race!
Aboon them a' ye tak your place, Painch, tripe, or thairm: Weel are ye wordy o' a grace As lang's my arm.
Address to a Haggis, Robert Burns 1786

Well we all know that haggis comes from Scotland but you should no more ask what is in it than you would ask a Highlander what is under his kilt. In either event you may get a nasty surprise.

There is no point in giving out a recipe because there is no point in attempting to make it yourself.
It is an ugly business and the same families have been making it for hundreds of years so you don't have to.
Make sure that you get a good one, made the old way, but you don't have to go far.
MacSween is probably the most popular brand but no less for it. In a blind tasting they won outright.
Waitrose and other posh retailers sell it; they even do a vegetarian version, god forbid.

Now put it to good use and pay its forefathers some due respect.
As a stuffing in any 'timorous beastie' it works wonders,
Haggis Scotch Eggs swap the sausage jacket. The original creators of Scotch Eggs, Fortnum & Mason sell them.
Try replacing the usual porcini duxelles in Beef Wellington with the stuff and you will be loved.
Or just fry a slice and pair it with its sibling, black pudding.
With neeps and tatties on the side, you'll be lifting your kilt and showing us if you 'are or not' in no time.

Although the most dedicated aficionado of blood sausages would never claim Scotland as the originators, it can rightly hold its head high with some of the finest. Stornoway Black Puddings, from the Isle of Lewis in the Western Isles of Scotland are the only ones ever to have been recognised with EU's Protected Geographical Indicator of Origin (PGI), quite an honour. Made to a unique recipe with clearly defined list of ingredients, unlike most puddings they use sheep's blood as well as the more traditional pigs'.

The two main suppliers up there have been friendly rivals for 75 years and share a common surname as, in fact, do most other residents of the island. Well they don't get over to the mainland often. Charles MacLeod Ltd has been in business since the end of WW2 yet considered a young upstart compared to MacLeod & MacLeod, 1931.

Both are still family run and I wouldn't dare make a comparison of their products. Both are some of the finest black puddings I have tasted and I have tried a lot all over the world. Both families run a mail-order service direct from the Western Isles that I can vouch for.

No discussion on black pudding would be complete without mention of Clonakilty, my all-time favourite breakfast slice. When I used to travel to Cork I would drop by the Clonakilty shop in the airport to fill my bags and fill my boots. The only other shop in the place was Barry's Tea, another classic. That filled the other bag.

La Morcilla

La Morcilla, Black Pudding, Boudin Noir, Buristo, call it what you will but it has one thing in common - pig's blood and that has to come from a pig. Blood is quite tricky to work with and the best morcilla are made by hand with fresh blood straight from the live animal or at least an animal that has just been slaughtered, otherwise the blood coagulates. Much commercial product is made with powdered blood reconstituted into liquid.

In the Spanish countryside, at the end of Autumn, family and friends gather one early morning for they have a date with death. It is time for La Matanza, the ritual slaughter of the family pig to produce food for the coming winter months. A roving butcher tours the farmsteads to provide this service. It is a particular skill. Ideally the animal has to be calm or adrenalin will get into the muscle and toughen it. Try telling that to the pig.

By the time the butcher arrives much drinking has been done already, It would depend on the region but it is generally spirit of some sort. As hardened as these old buggers pretend, the manic squeal of the pig, if he cottons on to his imminent fate, can put a chill down their spines.

The beast is laid along the table, all the while being massaged and stroked, Swiftly the main artery is cut and the blood is drained out into a bucket. While the men stay and help with the butchering, the women take the blood elsewhere to make Morcilla only returning a while later to claim some lard for their preparations.

Augments as to the recipe between the matriarchs are as much a ritual as the slaughter. The blood is mixed with various spices then fresh diced pig fat together with, depending on the style, either rice or onions and possibly some pine nuts depending on the region. Meanwhile the intestines have been washed by the younger women who aren't up to the fight. These are stuffed (the intestines, not the girls) with the mixture and tied off with hemp cord to make long strings. Lowered into a cauldron of boiling water for ten minutes or so the blood will now coagulate and firm. The morcilla is finished hanging outside in the sun.

Now the old biddies can have a drink too.

On Mince and

Many cultures have their own version of stewed mince, albeit some with different meats and flavouring. Bolognese, Picadillo, Keema, Ragu, call it what you like.

- Stuff it in cabbage leaves in France and you have Chou Farci.
- In China they have Minchi, heavy with soy sauce.
- The British make it with beef into Cottage Pie with a mash topping, or as Shepherds Pie using lamb.
- The Aussies put it in pastry and just call it Meat Pie.
- In Turkey mince is wrapped in grape leaves to make Dolma.
- Chili con Carne adds chilli and possibly pinto or kidney beans.
- Layer it with pasta and the Italians give you Lasagne.
- Layer it with aubergine, top it with Bechamel and you have Greek Moussaka.

All are different but the basics given here are very similar and good technique makes the most of it.

Me? I grew up with mince on toast, still my go to childhood comfort food.

And here is the bonus; this works for any protein to make a good stew. Try chicken thighs, rabbit, pig cheeks, diced pork, firm silken tofu, even fish like monkfish or mackerel, although just add it 20 minutes before the end of cooking.

Ingredients for a general meat Ragu

- 1 kg 50/50 mixed ground pork and beef
- 250 g chicken liver (optional)
- 1 kg onions, diced
- 5 cloves of fresh garlic, chopped
- 250 g Tomate Frito
- 5 or 6 tinned anchovies
- slug of Lea & Perrins
- slug of Tabasco
- 2 cubes of crumbled chicken stock
- 3 tbsp each of dried oregano & thyme
- 1 tbsp sweet paprika
- 1 tbsp curry powder (more if you want a curry)
- 1 bottle of drinkable wine

OTHER MEATS

Ask your butcher to make fresh mince. Use chuck steak, brisket and pork shoulder but take her advice.

Use a cast iron heavy bottomed Dutch oven like Le Creuset. Lidl make a great copy only much cheaper.

In there soften onions and garlic very, very slowly on a minimal heat until they first get transparent and finally caramelise but do not burn.Toast your spices before they get wet, ideally in a dry pan or add them to the onions, once done, for a few minutes, before adding anything else.

Brown your meat in very small batches, maximum of 200 g at a time. Use a heavy cast iron pan if you have one. Get it very hot on the highest gas. Allow it to reheat between batches. Break the mince up like you were making cement then push it around until it is even. Leave it alone until you can smell it browning then flip it all over. Don't fiddle around. Decant each batch to a bowl until your onions are ready.

When you have browned all the meat deglaze the pan with a little stock or wine into the pot, to get the wonderful caramel that has stuck to the bottom. Repeat until the pan is clean.

With the pan is still hot boil the wine, swilling it around, a bit at the time, to remove all the alcohol or it will make the dish bitter.

Add anchovies to the beef for a stronger flavour.

Finally put all the ingredients in the pot and add more liquid until it is just showing below the top of the stew, give it a stir, stick the lid on, and pop in the oven at 140C for a very long time.

It will be ready when you think it is.

Serve with rice, mash, lentils, on toast, anything to soak up all that lovely juice.

You may need a nap afterwards but leave it out on the stove to pick at in the middle of the night.

PA AMB TOMAQUET

Pa amb tomàquet (Pan con tomate in Spanish) is the epitome of every Catalan table, though you may see it elsewhere in the country as 'pan tumaca'.

At the simplest level you could translate it as 'bread with tomato' yet it is far more involved than that. There is a ritual that accompanies it.

Traditionally a basket of dry toasted bread is presented together with whole garlic cloves and halved tomatoes on a small saucer. Already on the table there would be a condiment set of olive oil, vinegar and salt.

You take a garlic clove, skin it, and scrape it across the bread. This is where it instantly fails for me as I watch the inner bread crumble and collapse until I am left with nothing but a ring of crust and a still intact clove. Obviously I am too heavy handed especially if the garlic is not very fresh as it should be or the toast too soft.

The tomato is next brought to bare, the open side of which is rubbed across the bread, squeezing it slightly to release the juices. Over this salt is sprinkled then a generous drizzle of olive oil.

Unless I am in someone's home, where manners come first, this guiri (rather pejorative slang for a vulgar foreigner) feels that at a restaurant there's a chef behind the pass who should be doing all the preparation, not the customer, and that includes the Pa amb Tomàquet.

Many bars now do just that, though it is made in a much more simple, frankly reliable, way and prepared in advance thus:

- Take a bunch of small vine tomatoes and coarsely blend them with an immersion blander.
- If you are being really lazy you can substitute a packet of tomàquet fregit (tomate frito) though this can be rather runny for the purpose.
- Either way, to the tomato paste add pre-diced garlic, a staple of every Catalan freezer, and whoosh it all up, slowly drizzling olive oil in as you go.
- Salt to taste.

Now all you need do is smear this on fresh toast with a pastry brush or, as is usual in bars, a household paint brush. I know I may get labelled with much untranslatable abuse but it is a bloody sight more practical than ripping bread to pieces. Give it a go and see or tell the chef to do some work.

Cochinillo

It's piggies ....
Every year, when I went back to the UK for Christmas, I would buy a frozen Cochinillo, what you might know as a Suckling Pig, from one of the better stores and pack it in my carry-on suitcase. It came vacuum sealed. All curled up it looked rather sweet and cosy.

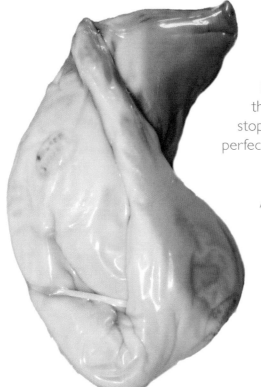

At Spanish airport security I'd dash through to try and catch my little chum in the case on the x-ray scanner. I was rather hoping that it would look like a small child. I never did see him but nobody stopped me. Why would they? A man taking a pig home to his family is perfectly natural here in Catalonia.

And perfect for Christmas it is too. Does anyone really like a dry old bird like turkey; there is a good reason they are served but once a year. Just the sight of a whole golden roasted pig brought to the table aloft brings sleigh-bells a-ringing.

What size to buy involves a bit of guesswork. It needs to fit in your oven but you want enough to feed the table, Luckily the meat is so rich then you don't necessarily need much for each guest but you can guarantee that there won't be any left. Simply put, get the biggest that you can wedge in your oven. If it is a small one (about 50 l) then 4/5 kg, for a huge oven (90 l) a beast of 8/9 kg should feed a large gathering. If you can only fit a baby then jam a load of sausage stuffing surrounding a pork loin inside and sew it up with butcher's string.

As grand as it looks it really is quite difficult to cock up cooking a cochinillo. It is barely worth a recipe but try this.

Allow your little feller to warm up out of the fridge then generously grease him all over with butter or lard and rub in coarse salt. If you are going to stuff it then now is the time. I won't give a recipe here as everyone has grandma's own, but make it sweet and boozy by including rum soaked apricots and raisins.

Tightly wrap the tail, ears and snout in tin foil. Stick a tangerine in his mouth.

Lay him out in an oven dish, longways or on his side. If he's a really big bugger then you'll just have to cram him in the oven alone and put a dripping tray below. Turn the oven to about 140°C and go to the pub for a few pints.

Give it about 4 hours, you can't really bugger it up, then pull all the tin foil off the ears etc and crank up the volume to 250°C for half-an-hour to really crisp up the skin. If you have a temperature probe it should be about 72°C deep in the front shoulder.

Take the boy out and lay him on a large serving dish or a wooden board. Trying not to break up the meat, gently remove the stuffing and set aside. At this stage grab at least one of the ears for yourself: Chef's treat!

Let him rest for 5/10 minutes then ceremonially march him to the table. It is said that, if done right, you can cut it up with a plate. Personally I prefer either a hefty cleaver to portion it out or just let everyone roll up their sleeves and start ripping at the beast with their hands like vultures at a carcass.

Bones Festes

Brain Food

The Apocalyptic chant of the Zombies:
What do we want? ... BRAINS!
When do we want them? ... BRAINS!
Well I want brains now too and I'm going to having some.

It is strange how, even for lovers of offal, many find brains challenging.
Strange, considering it has to be the most pure of any organ in the body and the most delicate.
Brains contain omega 3 fatty acids and are high in nutrients include phosphatidylcholine and phosphatidylserine, which, funnily enough, are good for the nervous system.
When eaten they remind me most closely of a savoury version of my childhood pleasure, Angel Delight.

Even many pescatarians take great pleasure in sucking the brains from out of the head of a prawn but suggest animal brain to many hardened carnivores and they go weak at the knees, scared that they might turn into one of the undead. Yet they are savoured all over the world in many cuisines.

If you are prepared to give it a go, there are classic ways before trying the more abstruse.

Sesos de Cordero a la Romana
Lamb's brain is broken into tablespoon size pieces, soaked in milk, breaded then quickly deep-fried. To remove yourself from the process I would recommend starting at Can Vilaro in San Antoni, Barcelona. They have them on the menu every day ('Cervell a la Romana' in Catalan) and are the best I've had. All light and fluffy it is more about texture than taste.

Cervelle de Veau au Beurre Noisette
The classic French way, Calf Brains are sautéed in brown butter and capers. This gives them a lovely nutty taste which brings out the best of the naturally subtle flavour. When they first opened the lovely Clipstone Restaurant, just behind Broadcasting House, had them on the daily lunch menu. They were perfectly prepared in true French style. It felt like the restaurant was making a statement of their intentions. Sadly they took them off and I haven't been since but do go anyway. They produce some fine fare nonetheless.

Omelete de Mioleira
A Portuguese dish of pork brains cooked with eggs. The brains are cut up in pieces, fried then mashed up. The pan is taken off the heat and whisked eggs are stirred in so the whole dish is creamy. I would say it is more scrambled egg than omelette. Americas in the Midwest used eat a similar dish for breakfast, no fancy name, just Brain and Egg. It was cheap and popular in hard times. Apparently it's making a bit of a comeback now.

RECIPE FOR CERVELLE DE VEAU AU BEURRE NOISETTE - Calf Brain in brown butter

Very carefully remove the membrane from the brain and soak it in 50/50 milk & water for a hour.

Make a court-bouillon by boiling celery, carrots, leek, onion, a bay leaf and whatever you have lying about in a litre of water. The green tops of leeks that you may otherwise throw away are excellent for this.
After 30/40 minutes strain into another pan. This is your poaching liquid. Bring to a low simmer so it is barely bubbling.

Take the brain from where it has been soaking and gently lower it into the court-bouillon with a large slotted spoon. Poach for 20 minutes then carefully pat dry with a clean tea-towel. Note kitchen roll may leave bits of paper behind.

While poaching take 200g of butter and melt it in a cast iron pan over a medium heat. Let it foam but keep stirring to get the milk solids from the bottom. It will start to brown and give off a nutty aroma. Once browned stir in a good slug on cider vinegar. Add 80g of drained capers and keep warm.

At this point some choose to sauté the brains in the butter for a few minutes. However it is a delicate operation and not absolutely necessary. Either way now place the brain on a slice of toast or fried bread and pour the brown butter over it. Sprinkle with finely chopped fresh parsley and salt to taste.

EGG vs. EGG

To some there seems to be little difference between scrambled eggs and an omelette but they could not be further apart. Have a look and see if you could up your game.

SCRAMBLED EGG

You really need to get ready for this one because, if you do it right, you are going to be hanging around for a long time and one little distraction will ruin the whole process. Go to the loo, check you messages, turn the phone off and the radio on.

Before you start on the eggs make some toast. It might be cold by the time you have finished but the hot eggs will warm it up again. When the toast is done immediately butter it so it melts into the toast. This will stop it drying out. Marmite might be a good addition if you're not one of those weird haters. Do not leave this until the end. This is just the kind of distraction that will ruin your eggs at the crucial point. If you are going for bacon, get this in motion too.

Get a heavy bottomed pan and put it on your lowest heat. If you have gas use your smallest burner and the lowest flame possible. If induction or, god forbid, electric, try it at about a 3.
Straight away drop in at least 100g of butter and push it around the pan. You just want it to melt and stay melted without burning. If it starts to brown pull the pan away; you have the heat too high already. If it stays solid you have forgotten to turn the hob on.

Meanwhile get three eggs (you took them out of the fridge half an hour ago, didn't you?) and crack them into a bowl. With a large pronged fork or chopsticks just start to break them up. Importantly do not whisk them. You are looking to get the yolk and white mixed in while still being able to distinguish bits of each. Think Jackson Pollock, Once it looks right add a drop of cold milk and a pinch of salt and stir a bit more.

How is the butter looking? Still just sitting melted in the pan? Good. Grab a wide silicone spatula. You are going to pour the mix into the pan but, crucially, the butter is not there to sauté the eggs in. It serves to make it all rich and buttery so as soon as you have them in start pushing the liquid away from the bottom of the pan to blend the butter in. If the eggs start to brown at all you have the heat too high. If so take the pan off the heat but carry on stirring. Did I mention that it has to be on low?

Now the test of patience begins. Push it slowly around and shovel across the top as if you are making cement. Do you know how to make cement? We are talking about a good 10 minutes plus so I hope you've got a good playlist on. Keep watching. Do not answer the phone. Finally the eggs will start to turn sloppy but slightly firmer. Move the pan away from the heat but leave the gas on. Now watch them. They should carry on cooking from the heat of the pan. If need be slide the pan back over the heat but just for a few seconds. When they look just slightly runnier that you would like them spoon them on to the toast and relax. Both you and the eggs. You did good. Tuck in.

*SCOTCH WOODCOCK

For a posh and ancient variation from the 19th century try Scotch Woodcock. Once served in the House of Commons and at Oxbridge colleges as an after-dinner savoury, buttered toast is lightly spread with Gentleman's Relish, a British anchovy paste. Take great note of the suggestion, or rather warning, as you open the jar. 'Use sparingly' it reads. Take heed. Pile your scrambled egg on top and dress with a single anchovy fillet and finely chopped parsley.
The late Prince Phillip used to cook it for himself as a late night snack.
Fergus Henderson recommends serving it with a shot of Fernet Branca but then he would, wouldn't he.

OMELETTES

Put a cast iron frying pan on the hottest heat. It will need to be there for a good while.

Crack two eggs into a bowl and hand-whisk. You are aiming to get a lot of air into them so put you back into it. You have plenty of time before the pan is hot enough. Add a good splash of oil in with a teaspoon of butter to the pan. Let the oil heat up. It should start to smoke but not burn. Pour in the egg in a spiral from the centre outwards, give it a swirl then bash the pan on the hob just once. If large bubbles form give them a whack then push some of the still liquid egg downwards. You must fold the omelette while it is still runny on top. The heat will continue cooking it from the inside even on the plate. Push down on the folded omelette. Some liquid should ooze out. Bash the pan on the hob again then ease the omelette onto a hot plate. Dress with chives or other fresh herbs.

Thirty seconds, one paragraph, job done. See the difference.

F.U.N.E.X?

BOILED EGGS must be the most perfect form. You just need to get it right.

When I was in the Netherlands as a kid we ordered a picnic to take to the park. Upon cracking a boiled egg I discovered the yolk was runny but not before dripping it down my front. Further, more careful, examination revealed them to be all to be as such . Apparently the good citizens of Holland like their cold boiled eggs soft, and I am in accord. Hard boiled eggs seem such a waste and leave a dry pasty feeling on the palate. Just warn your guests.

Ignore what you read about cold water. It is crucial that you put the eggs in hot but barely boiling water. If not the white will stick to the shell and they will be very difficult to peel.

Use warm eggs and make sure you have plenty of water or your timing can go out as the eggs could cool the water. A good thumb rule is 500 ml of water to each egg.

So how long? Well it obviously depends how you want them.

For a soft yolk time 6 minutes and whip them out swiftly though if you are inclined to faff around and don't have everything ready make that 5 and a faff. For hard-boiled go for 11-12, faffing dependant.

If you are going to eat them later, immediately shock them in a bowl of iced water for 10 minutes or they will continue to cook. If you are about to eat them now for breakfast whip the top off and stick them in an eggcup toot-suite. If you don't have egg cups shot glasses from the bar make a good stand-in.

A pinch of salt on top and don't forget the soldiers; a whole slice of toast is for draft-dodgers, not heroes.

The Marmite is something only you can decide.

THE SHAPE OF EGGS TO COME

Let us, for one moment consider the shape of an egg. It cannot have any corners so it should be a sphere but in that case the nucleus would always have maximum contact with the shell. An ellipse must be better for then for if stored upright the narrower ends would support the centre leaving some packaging beneath. The problem then being it would always roll away on the slightest incline, its centre of gravity being at the widest point. An ovoid does not have this issue. Its centre of mass is behind the point of contact towards the wider end. Therefore it sits with the nose tilted downwards. If you place it on a slight incline it may start to roll but will soon come to rest, the nose pointing up the slope. The perfect shape.

"But what about the poor chicken?" you may ask,

That will come later ...

36

Eggs fucking Benedict

What is it about 'brunch' that brings out the worst in the chattering classes? Is it the release from the ardours of a day job, when the weekend dawns and they all rush out at the earliest opportunity to knock back overpriced, over-proof cocktails posing as healthy fruit smoothies at 11 o'clock on a Saturday morning before they have sobered up from their ghastly Friday night piss-up with work colleagues, most of whom they can't stand to be with? It is this sort who sneer at old gits like myself who choose to go for a midweek morning pint at the local Spoons partly, I confess, because we can and they cannot. Strangely the main complaint against Wetherspoons, after the age of the average punter, is that it is very cheap, preferring to pay fifteen quid for the same gin and tonic just because the hipster barman, sorry mixologist, in a bow tie pours the measure out the back of his hand, not the front as if he cannot bend his wrist forwards from tossing himself off in front of a mirror too often. I'll take three pints of very decent ale against your one bottle of Peroni with a lemon stuck in the neck any day of the working week.

So how do eggs fit into this, you may well ask. Well ask any chef who has just pulled the dreaded Saturday or Sunday morning Brunch service, right after a long night's shift before. Eggs Benedict is the problem and bloody poached eggs are the culprit. He has to get up at silly o'clock with the prospect of prepping a 100 or more of the buggers for a bunch of tits pissed up on foul Prosecco while his lovingly prepared Hollandaise sauce splits in the heat of the kitchen.

How long does it take you to poach just a couple of eggs yourself on Sunday morning, if you can at all, just to soak your muffin in boiling water while ladling a load of wispy trails of egg white and a lump of solid yolk on top? Actually not long at all and you might even get it right in the process. Let me tell you how.

First pour yourself a gin and tonic. Nothing hefty, just a 50ml measure in a pint glass with lots of tonic and a few drops of cucumber bitters. You're thirsty, hungover and need refreshing but you cannot do this pissed or you should go back to bed. Certainly not a Bloody Mary. You are about to eat runny eggs covered in a buttery egg sauce. Mix that with acidic tomato juice curdling around in your gut and you'll never make it to the pub afterwards.

Before you take a sip take your eggs out of the fridge. You need them at room temperature when you cook them. It is not recommended that you even keep them in there but, let's face it, everyone does.

Get one teacup for each egg, lay clingfilm across the top and push it down inside. Crack each egg into a fine mesh sieve and gently swirl it around over the sink. You will see some goo come through. It is at this point that you learn that there are two parts to the egg white. You are getting rid of the outer more watery part. Whether you can really be bothered with this is up to you. Put an egg into each lined teacup, add a tiny pinch of salt then twist the film to seal in the eggs, excluding as much air as possible. Get a large pan of water and bring it to the boil ready for when you need it. Turn it off, stick a lid on and have a good slurp. You may as well slot your bread or muffin in the toaster all ready to toast. If you're going to have bacon then now is the time to cook it. Personally I prefer a slice of Serrano ham and it is a lot easier. We're prepped up and good to go. Time to make the Hollandaise.

Take 3 large fresh eggs and separate the yolks from the white. Try and get as little white in the yolk as possible. Set the whites aside in the fridge. You'll want those for the Pisco Sours when you get back from the pub. Drop the yolks in an upright blender. You can use an immersion blender but you will have that in one hand and a jug of boiling butter in the other. What are you going to hold the bowl with, your dick?

To the eggs add a squirt of lemon juice from that plastic fruit in the fridge, a good dollop of English mustard (not that French bird's shit) and a pinch of salt. Put the top on, but leave the bung out, and blast it for 20 seconds or so, just enough for it blend together.

Chop 250 gm of unsalted butter into chunks and put in a Pirex jug. Cover with clingfilm and pop into the microwave, initially for a minute then increments of 10 seconds. It is crucial that it is really, really hot or this will not work. When you think it must be hot enough give it another blast. Just try not to burn it.

With a kitchen towel remove the hot jug and get the blender, with your eggs, running at a medium speed then start to drizzle the butter in at a very gentle pace through the hole in the lid. Do not accelerate towards the end just because it is going well or you'll bugger it up. If you do, carry on until the butter is finished.

Fuck, You split it!
Fear not. In the blender slowly add a dash boiling water from the kettle,
a tablespoon at a time. If that doesn't work try another egg yolk.
If still no joy just get on with the rest and
be grateful you didn't bring anyone
home last night to see you
crying. It will still taste the
same as long as you
keep the salty
tears out of
it.

Here
we go
then.
Hit the toaster. You do not
want to finish your eggs before you have
something to put them on. Turn the pan of water back on and bring it back up to
where you can just see a few bubbles, no more.
185C is the perfect water temperature if you have a probe and can be arsed.

Take your clingfilmed eggs, lower them in by the tail and pop the lid back on. At this point you can turn the heat off unless you are cooking a large batch. Check your eggs after exactly 3 minutes. The white should be completely opaque. Lift them out with a slotted spoon catching any drips with a clean tea towel, snip off the tail and place on the awaiting toast. Lay a slice of ham on top each egg, not underneath where it would cover the toast leaving it dry, protecting it from the goodness seeping in from above. Now smother with Hollandaise. Don't be shy. Nothing should peek out. Generously grate good black pepper over it, add a few flakes of sea salt and a pinch of paprika.

You did it. Congratulations. Pour yourself a glass of that dry Riesling from the fridge you'd opened in readiness and raise a glass to those poor bastards in restaurant kitchens across Albion who already had to do that a hundred times this morning.
See you in the Spoons.

The Curate's Egg

No wonder fairy tales refer to the golden egg. That viscous little orb is the money shot of an egg; the rest is just packaging. If you are left with whites it is time for meringues or Pisco Sours. With the yolk you're spoilt for choice.

Cured Egg Yolks

These rich little babies are just a wonderful addition to pasta, soup or anything you might otherwise grate cheese on. Make a dry cure of half and half, salt & sugar. Mix well. You'll need enough to come half way up your container. Let's say 500g of each. Maybe add some pepper and even dried cumin but don't get carried away. This is about the egg.

You can do as many eggs as you have space for but let's start with six. You will need a shallow dish that will hold them with plenty of space around. Pour in half the mix and level out it out. Take a whole egg in its shell and make an indentation for each egg. Crack an eggs, separate the yolk and slide it into an indentation. If you break it shovel it out and try afresh. Repeat. When you've done them all gradually sprinkle the other half of the cure over until completely buried. Cover with clingfilm or a lid and pop in the fridge.

After 3 or 4 days carefully excavate them and brush off most of the salt. They will be firm with a slight give. Lay them out on baking paper. If you have a dehydrator and you're in no hurry pop them in there. Otherwise put them in the oven on the lowest possible temperature for 30 minutes. They should be firm and solid.

With a microplane grate a little off. You should taste the richness of the egg, almost buttery, a bit umami and a tad funky. Try on fresh plain pasta, over salad, soup, anywhere you might use grated Parmesan. Wasn't it worth the wait? The eggs will keep in the fridge for a month if you can keep your hands off them. You'll wish you had done more. Next time try with duck or goose eggs too. Larger eggs may take a little longer and can get a little funkier in a good way.

EGG CAPPUCCINO

Around the late 70s I used to go to the wine auctions of Sotheby's and Christie's. It was a great deal. For a small annual fee one could subscribe to the catalogue for the wine sales then, each week on Tuesday and Thursday mornings respectively, you would be invited to the auctions. It was up to the seller but there were always bottles out for tasting and these could be of the finest order. Once a year or so there would be a special sale, the most memorable of these was for the cellars of Mentmore Towers following the death of the 6th Earl of Rosebery. The tasting was held in the ballroom of the Cafe Royal. Being an estate sale the executors had put up bottles of every wine and what bottles there were. Chateau d'Yquem, Romanée-Conti, Pétrus, Château Latour, Château Margaux, Château Lafite, vintage Krug, Taylor's port to name just some, many of several vintages amongst hundreds of lots. The problem was that after a good few of these your pallet is lost and I was certainly not going to spit out any of that liquid gold so quickly got understandably rather refreshed. I ended up, after the event had closed, sitting under a table hidden by overhanging table cloths with a top sommelier, guzzling first growth clarets by the neck while the waiters cleared the room. Happy days

Now you may well ask what this reprobate behaviour has to do with eggs and I shall tell you, After the weekly auction at Sotheby's in Bond Street I and couple of other wine lovers would sneak out the back door to an Italian Cafe in St. George St. There our order was always Smoked Salmon and Egg. Fredo, the governor, would crack a couple of eggs onto a metal jug and stick this straight under the hot milk spout of his chrome Gaggia coffee machine. Egg foam would spew over the top of the jug and be poured over a decent serving of salmon with a good grinding of black pepper from one of those food tall Italian pepper towers. So light and fluffy, he called it scrambled egg but scrambled it was not. It was almost an instant soufflé but, for lack of anything else, I'm calling it Egg Cappuccino. Gorgeous.

Ferran Adria's Crisps Tortilla

The story goes that one of the chefs at El Bulli, Ferran Adrià's now legendary restaurant in Roses, was tasked with knocking up a post service snack for the team. He was completely knackered so just grabbed a pack of crisps and a few eggs and made this in minutes. Ferran was knocked out by this innovation and subsequently published a recipe in his book, Cocinar en Casa (Cooking at Home), claiming authorship for himself. My guess is that kids have been doing this for years. What Spanish kid would not love the idea of combining his favourite brand of 'chips' (what the English would call crisps) with a tortilla. Crisps are often served on the side anyway,

It is difficult to even consider it a recipe really but let's have a go.

Take a packet of your favourite crisps. Cheap old fashioned thin ones work better, or at least faster, than posh kettle chips if you're in a hurry The thick cut ones need soaking longer in the egg or they will remain determinedly hard rather that get mushed up in the goo.

So whisk up 8 or so large eggs with, optionally, finely chopped Serrano ham, chopped canned piquillo peppers, and some thyme leaves. No need to salt as this will come from the crisps themselves. Personally I would leave out all the extras and let the flavour of the chosen crisps decide the taste. Anything more than egg and crisps seems rather pretentious in this context.

Stir a bag of your favourite crisps into the eggs so they are all covered and wait 5 to 10 minutes.
Get a well oiled cast iron pan pretty hot and tip the mix in. Push it to the edge but then do not stir at all. Wait 3-4 minutes for the bottom to brown. At this point, If you are brave enough, flip the tortilla. Otherwise shift the pan to beneath a hot grill to cook the top for another 3-4 minutes. It is important that the inside is still moist and a tad sloppy. Remember that it will continue cooking on the plate.
Slice in triangles from the centre out, or cut into 3cm cubes with a toothpick in each.

Does anyone really like coffee?

No, really. I realise that it could be a controversial question but it can be disgusting muck a lot of the time and yet nobody seems to notice. I assume that half the time they are just drinking it for the hit. Caffeine is a fine drug taken in moderation but perhaps we should all just start sniffing it like snuff. Then we can clear the high streets of those ubiquitous bland chain cafés and admit we just want a lift to wake us up.

In Spain I start my day, when I'm out and about, with a Trifásico, the three phases of the name being strong coffee, a dash of milk and a shot of spirit, in my case, Pujol, a local rum. Between the alcohol and the caffeine it serves as a bit of a heart starter. I keep thinking that I really should cut out the booze but I enjoy the hit from the coffee. I tried it rum free and realised quite how disgusting the coffee was. The rum served to mask the taste and my breakfast was inedible without it. So why is this bitter concoction so popular?

The Chinese have never really had a coffee culture. In 1999 Starbucks opened in Beijing and later embedded one right in the Great Wall. Every time I went past I could see empty tables with full cups left stranded. The locals wanted to participate in this western ideology but couldn't actually stand the stuff so they would buy a cup and just dump it.

Who the hell first gathered the fresh beans and decided to burn them, grind them up into powder and pour hot water on, thus making a gritty mud which they drunk? It is generally agreed that coffee consumption originated in Ethiopia where, about 1,000 years ago, they'd neck the fresh coffee cherries like pill-heads at the Hacienda or pulped them to make dough with goat fat. That must have been a lively bakers. It was only much later, in the Yemen, that the cultivated seeds were first roasted, ground and drunk in hot water so sorry Italians, you didn't invent it. My theory is that the Arabs made fires from goat shit and realised that the crap from the goats that had been chomping on the coffee cherries was decidedly aromatic so got stuck in. In Indonesian you get Kopi Luwak, coffee made from partially digested cherries found in the poo of the Asian palm civets, the bean fermenting as it passes through the beast. I have drunk it and it is mild, very smooth and has a beautiful flavour, although I wouldn't fancy harvesting it myself; a truly shit job.

The coffee bean is not a bean at all but the seed of a fruit, the coffee cherry. These start green then ripen until they are red. There is very little flesh in the fruit, just a tough skin surrounding one or most likely two seeds, a single seed being a Peaberry. At this point the pulp still adheres to the seeds like an apricot or mango does. Commercially, as the first process towards your morning pick-me-up, the skin is removed and the seeds are soaked in a water bath for a couple of days so the pulp can soften and can be removed. Preferably you may find 'natural processed coffee' a superior product where the fruit has been dried whole or 'honey processed', the fruit skinned but the pulp left on. The 'mucilage', the sticky pulp, slightly ferments, thus giving the coffee a fruitier taste. Either way the seeds are dried, usually just in the sun and become the 'beans' we know.

After all this the beans are sent out for roasting and this is where I have issues. On the way from my old flat in Old Compton Street to the office in Brewer Street I would pass, or rather enter, the Algerian Coffee Shop opposite, drawn by the beautiful aromas wafting down the street. Here they have some of the finest beans from around the globe, roasted in-house to whichever level you wished. What I fail to understand if why anyone would want to take these aromatic gorgeous seeds and burn the buggery out of them for high roast Espresso, effectively turning them to finely ground soot, just to stick it in a three grand fancy chrome steam machine, the resulting nasty liquid bitter and burnt.

Please go there or your local purveyors and ask them to recommend something smooth. Specify medium roast, medium ground. If you don't have a French press, and you should, use an old jug. Ladle in a couple of tablespoonfuls of your golden powder. Pour in hot water, just slightly off the boil. You wouldn't want to scald your precious beans at this point. Stir once. Give it five minutes then filter through fine muslin into a thick white china mug. If you so wish add a tiny splash of cold milk, certainly not that foamy nonsense. Now go sit by the window and spark one up if you so do. Enjoy the moment. The caffeine will kick in shortly and you can crack on with the day ahead. Cheers.

45

SOME RECIPES

Esparragos de Ajo Blanco

Although possibly Roman, Ajo Blanco is a cold soup traditionally considered Andalusian.
Here it is thickened and used as a sauce.

Although now available all year round, the peak season for asparagus is spring, and at its best then.
Personally I prefer the very fine early crop and certainly never those white logs. They are Satan's turds and should be confined to wherever white dog poo disappeared to in the 80s.

For a real treat pick them fresh from a garden and eat within half an hour,
You will need a handful of fresh green asparagus, bottom ends trimmed off, for each guest.

Salsa:

- 2 Cloves garlic
- 1 tbsp Jerez vinegar
- ½ cup Toasted almonds
- ½ cup Ice water.
- ½ cup Extra virgin olive oil.
- Dried or stale bread, soaked in a little water or milk

First blend the almonds to a fine powder then add garlic, vinegar, and water. With the blender running at the slowest speed, carefully drizzle in the oil in a fine stream.

Use more oil if it is too thick.
Add the bread to smooth it.

To cook the asparagus for a large party:
Preheat oven to 200°C
Wash the asparagus and shake excess water off. Lay each still wet bunch on sheet of tin foil and drizzle some olive oil on the tips. Add salt and pepper.
Wrap foil across the top and crinkle to seal.
Put in the oven for 8 minutes.

Otherwise, if cooking a small amount, just steam until tender.

Remove the asparagus from the foil and line up on a plate. Pour a strip of the sauce over the top end of the asparagus, but leaving the very tips exposed.

Dress with toasted almonds, black garlic and salt flakes.

Vitello Tonnato

Although Italian, specifically Piedmontese, in origin I think of this as a classic Mar i Montana Catalan combination though rarely seen here.

Many years ago I used to go to Ciao Bella in Lambs Conduit Street just for this but, inexplicably, they took it off the menu and I never went back.

As your butcher for an Eye Round Fillet.
Vacuum pack the beef fillet along with mirepoix. Sous Vide for 48 hours at 55°C. Shock the sealed bag in a bath of ice and store it in the fridge. This will give you beautifully tender, melt in the mouth, pink beef.

Before using, rest in a freezer for 40 minutes.
This will enable you to finely slice it more easily.

Tonnato Sauce:

• 2 Egg yolks
• I Large garlic clove
• 2 tbsp Vinegar
• 75 g Canned tuna in olive oil
• 2 Anchovy fillets
• 2 tbsp Capers
• I tbsp Lemon juice
• 275 ml Good quality olive oil

Put egg yolks in a food processor with garlic and anchovies. With the processor running, very gently drizzle the oil in. Add vinegar, tuna, capers and lemon to taste.

Plate very thin slices of beef in a spiral.
Smear with Tonnato sauce.
Dress with fresh capers, boquerones, and fake caviare.

Tabbouleh

Levantine Tabbouleh is great kitchen standby, it can keep for a few days in the fridge, the flavours developing over time. A great accompaniment to grilled meats or just as a standalone vegetarian option.

Traditionally it is made with parsley but I have never quite understood the appeal of that herb in any form. Coriander has a much more pronounced and distinctive flavour but can be offensive to some palates so check with your guests. Or you can even use Lovage if you can find some. Whichever way the herbs should be dominant.

- 250g Fine grade bulgur wheat
- Big bunch of mint
- Bunch of Coriander (substitute lovage if you can find it)
- 250 g Cherry or small plum tomatoes
- Spring Onions, finely chopped
- 250 g Seasonal soft fruit: Figs, peaches, plums, strawberries.
- 120 ml Strong spicy olive oil

Dice the fruit and soak in lemon juice, brown sugar and dark rum for a couple of hours then drain.

Chop the tomatoes into half or quarters depending on the size. Sprinkle with 50 g coarse salt, 50 g white sugar and a large tablespoon of dried Oregano. Mix well and leave for an hour. This will extract some water, concentrating the flavour and enhancing the taste. Rinse well in a coarse sieve until the dried herbs have cleared. Leave to dry.

Rinse the Bulgur Wheat until the water runs clear.
Soak in water for 45 minutes then drain well.
Leave in a fine sieve to dry for 30 minutes.
Pour oil over the wheat and mix well by hand.

Pull mint leaves from the stems and finely chop.
Remove the bottom third from a bunch of coriander (or pull leaves from Lovage) then rinse and coarsely chop, removing any excessively large stems.

Add tomatoes, fruit, spring onions, mint & coriander to the drained Bulgur wheat and mix in by hand.
Serve in a large sharing bowl with a few herb leaves scattered on top.

Chorizo and Prawns in Vermut

Often as not I have a couple of Chorizo knocking about in the fridge and a bag of frozen prawns in the freezer. I certainly have a bottle of Catalan Vermut in the house unless I drunk it the night before. Thereby I can knock a version of this up in 5 minutes when friends unexpectedly drop by, even if the coriander is missing. It is always well received though there is never any vermut left afterwards.

- A small onion or shallot and a clove of garlic, finely diced
- 120 g Chorizo, sliced
- Handful of frozen prawns
- 125 ml Vermut
- One stem of spring onion, chopped
- Shredded fresh coriander

Quickly fry onion and garlic in olive oil over a hot pan. Turn the heat down, add the chorizo and fry for a few minutes until the red oil from the chorizo begins to release.

Pour in a slug of vermut and let bubble then add the prawns. Reduce the vermut until thick and sticky and prawns have turned pink, about 5 minutes. Remove from the heat, stir in spring onion and coriander

Serve in a terracotta bowl with more vermut to drink on the side and fresh bread to mop the salsa with.

Bon Profit!

SPICY CAULIFLOWER AND CASHEW SOUP

This makes a surprising soup to start a meal or just as a pick-me-up. It can be served chilled in the summer in a glass with a cube of ice, or, in colder months, piping hot in a mug.

Either way place a blob of Lao Gan Ma's Spicy Chili Crisp on top. You can find it in any Asian Supermarket. You'll easily recognise it from the picture of "Old Grandmother", Tao Huabi, who invented it, on the jar. Just go easy!

- The head of a cauliflower, core cut out, chopped up
- 2 Bay leaves, a few stems of fresh thyme and a bunch of lovage if you can find it, tied into a bouquet garni
- 3 Onions, Figueres if you can get them, diced
  - 1 tbsp Minced garlic
  - Pinch of cayenne pepper
  - 1 tsp Paprika
  - 200 ml Dry white wine
  - 2 tsp Lemon juice
  - 120 g Raw cashew nuts
  - 1.5 litres Vegetable stock

Slowly sauté onions and garlic in olive oil until transparent to brown.
Add paprika & cayenne and stir for a few minutes.
Add wine and lemon juice and reduce it all by half.
Add the cauliflower, cashews and bouquet garni plus 300 ml stock.
Cook for 20/30 minutes on a low heat with a lid on the pan, stirring occasionally.
Discard bouquet garni, season then blend in stages adding the remaining stock as you go.
If serving cold let cool then rest in a fridge for a few hours.
Just don't forget Old Grandmother!

SMOKED TROUT AND HORSERADISH CREAM

Great for summer picnics or light lunches.

If you don't have a smoker this can be done in a wok or heavy pan.
Put the wood chips in the bottom then find a round metal rack that fits half way up.
Get the wood smoking on a low heat then quickly cover with a tight fitting lid or tin foil.

Wet brine:
• 200 cl Water
• 60g Coarse salt
• 60g White sugar
• 2 tbsp Soy sauce
• 3 tbsp Minced garlic and ginger
• 1 tbsp Fresh ground black pepper
• 1 tbsp Paprika
• 1 tbsp Dry thyme

Pin bone 2 large sea trout fillets (2 kg) or 4 smaller rainbow trout
Brine the trout for 2 hours maximum in food-safe seawater or use the salt brine above.
Rinse very well, pat with kitchen roll, then leave out to air dry for an hour.
Smoke at 80°C for 90 minutes

Remove the skin from the trout, checking for bones, then coarsely flake.
Combine with 250 ml of crème fraîche, a good dollop of hot horseradish sauce and a handful of finely chopped fresh dill.

Portion out into china bowls, dress with salmon or trout roe and a few fronds of fresh dill,
Serve with warm baguettes or crackers.

Welsh Rarebit IPA

A British staple for at least three hundred years, also know as Welsh Rabbit, so called to avoid any confusion with a real bunny, it contains no meat of any kind although Worcestershire sauce, an essential ingredient, does contain a touch of anchovy.

Traditionally the cheese is a strong Cheddar. We generally use a good quality Manchego Curado, others swear by Gruyère, but something with a bit of bite and tang is obligatory.

The beer is down to you but should be something decent and fairly heavy. Draft IPAs work very well. Some even prefer stout though it does give it a rather unappealing colour. Like cooking with wine, don't use anything you wouldn't want to drink. Ideally it should be served with that same beer.

Buck Rarebit is the same thing but with the addition of a poached egg atop.

Mix the mustard powder and Tara gum with the flour.
Melt butter in a pan and sift the flour mix in over a low heat until blended, continuously stirring.

Slowly pour beer into the roux, still stirring.
Add Worcestershire Sauce to the beer mix.
This will also prevent it splitting.

Put the cheese in, a bit at a time, with more stirring, on the very lowest heat until you have an even mixture. Turn the heat off before adding the last bit of cheese or it may split. Add Cayenne pepper and salt to taste.

Spread the warm mix on toasted bread and brown with an industrial blowtorch or under the grill.

Splash with a few more drops of Worcestershire Sauce, top with a thin slice of gherkin and a few chopped chives.

Serve with Piccalilli on the side.

- 100 g Butter
- 100 g Flour
- 3 tsp Colman's Mustard powder
- ½ tsp Cayenne pepper
- ½ tsp Tara gum (optional)
- 500 ml IPA Beer
- 500 g Grated cheddar
- 2 tsp Lea & Perrins
- Chopped chives for dressing

Japanese Seaweed Salad with Mojama and Pomegranate Dressing

'In truth, as any fool knows, seaweed looks and tastes like the pubic hair of a Rhinemaiden'
Will Self

Mojama is loin of tuna from Cadiz, cured in salt then left to dry out in the sun for a month. Very firm, it has to be sliced very finely. It is traditionally served drizzled in fine olive oil. The salad works equally well without it though. I put the dressing on everything.

- Packet of dried Japanese seaweed
- Lotus root in brine
- Pink sushi ginger
- Toasted sesame seeds
- English cucumber, sliced as finely as possible
- Mojama, hand sliced very thinly

Dressing
- 1/3 Seasoned rice vinegar
- 1/3 Pomegranate molasses
- 1/3 Sesame oil

Soak 30 g dried seaweed for 10 minutes.

Drain, squeeze and pat the seaweed dry.
Separately soak cucumber and seaweed in the dressing and layer in a serving bowl to make a pyramid.
Top with pink ginger & 4 stems of lotus root.
Dress with sesame seeds.

If required place some Mojama around the edge of the plate and drizzle it with good olive oil.

Upside-Down Leek Tart

Not just a great vegetarian substitute but a marvellous standalone afternoon tea or just as a starter. Be generous with the Parmesan.
Works well as a side dish for fish or meats too.

- Packet of puff pastry (keep in fridge until needed)
- 8 leeks, trimmed and split down the centre, lengthways
- 120 ml Balsamic vinegar
- 60 g Butter
- 2 tsp Sugar
- 2 tsp Fresh thyme
- 100 g Parmesan
- Dijon mustard.

Heat oven to 200°C
Toss leeks in olive oil, salt, and pepper and lay out on a baking sheet. Roast until tender, about 20 minutes. Remove the tough outer layer of each leek.

Meanwhile simmer the vinegar until slightly reduced. Add butter, sugar, and 1 tsp thyme, ideally fresh, until the butter has melted.

Pour vinegar mix on a baking sheet.
Arrange leeks, cut sides down and side by side, in rows,
Brush leeks with Dijon mustard.
Generously sprinkle with Parmesan.

Drape pastry over the leeks and tuck in the edges
Make a couple of slits in the pastry to let the steam escape. Put in the oven and bake until the pastry is dark brown, about 40 minutes.

Put a matching tray on top and flip over.
Season with thyme and sea saltflakes.

Magret d'Anec

- One duck breast for each couple
- Orange slices
- Chopped garlic
- Grated ginger
- Brown sugar
- Knob of butter
- Juice of one orange

Salad suggestions:
Fennel, thinly sliced on a mandolin, with segments of tangerine, pith removed
Or
Yellow chanterelles, sautéed in butter, rocket and fresh raspberries

Dressing for either salad:
- 1/3 Sesame oil
- 1/3 Sushi vinegar
- 1/3 Pomegranate molasses
Shake together well

Lightly score the skin diagonally two ways to make a diamond pattern. Try not cut into the surface of the meat. Crisp the fat side on a hot plancha to render the fat out (save the fat for roast potatoes and tortilla de patatas). Be careful not to burn it. Let cool then pat dry. Leave on paper towels to let any liquid drain out.

Mix garlic, ginger and brown sugar then coat the duck, pressing into the skin.
Vacuum seal individually together with an orange slice.
Sous Vide at 54.5°C (Minimum safe temperature) for a maximum of 4 hours.

If not serving immediately, remove from the water bath and shock in a bowl of iced water then store in the fridge. To reheat, return to the hot water bath for 10 minutes to bring it back up to temperature.

De-bag, saving any liquid, pat very dry, then briefly flash fat side on hot plancha again to crisp up the skin.
Wrap in tin foil and rest for 5 minutes.

Meanwhile, soften a knob of butter, mix with the reserved liquid and the juice of an orange and slightly reduce.

Once rested slice diagonally across, about 4mm wide, at a 30 degree angle.

Pour on juices and lightly scatter with flakes of salt.

Make a base of salad and place slices of duck on top.

Octopus Carpaccio

A most elegant party dish, easy to prepare in advance.
You will need a large octopus, about 2/3 kg.
You may be able to get the fishmonger to clean it.
If not get out your sharpest knife.

Cut off the head just below the eyes. Turn it inside out and remove all the innards. Detach the eyes: Pinch together the flesh surrounding the eyes, and neatly slice them off. Peel away the outer membrane. Slice the head in strips from top to bottom. Spread the tentacles to locate the beak. Cut around it and push it out from behind. Thoroughly rinse both head and tentacles.

Now put it all in a plastic bag and freeze overnight. This will both sterilise it and make the final dish more tender. Leave out to unfreeze and you are ready to cook it.

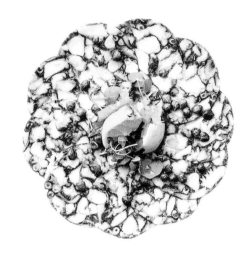

In a large pan bring salted water to the boil.
When on a rolling boil hold the tentacles by the body, dip into the water for a few seconds and withdraw, letting the water drain off. You will see the tentacles begin to curl. Repeat a few times until all the tentacles have curled up to your satisfaction. Then slowly lower the whole thing into the pan and add the strips of head. Turn the water to the lowermost simmer possible and leave for about an hour. It is done when you can insert a knife into the thickest part of the tentacles without much pressure. Turn the heat off and allow to cool in the cooking water. Drain and allow to cool further until it is barely warm. Cut the tentacles into singles.

Now on to the assembly:

Take an empty 2 litre plastic soft-drink bottle, the sort you get the lemonade for your Pimms in. Pierce a hole in the centre of the base and cut the top off below the pointy bit.
In turn drop each tentacle into the bottle and push down with large wooden spoon or potato masher if it fits, squeezing as much liquid out through the hole in the base. Between each tentacle sprinkle with paprika and add a couple of bits of the head .

When full make a few cuts in the bottle from the top down to where the octopus starts. Fold these over inwards to create a top, trimming the strips to fit the width of the bottle. Wrap the bottle in cling film and pop in the freezer.

When ready to serve cut away the cling film and bottle and you should have a frozen cylinder of octopus. Slice very finely with a mandolin or sharp knife.

Place the slices in a spiral on a serving plate and add a touch more paprika. Serve with a warm potato salad on the side.

Tongue Vinaigrette

Whole ox tongue

Salad:
- 1 Mango or paw paw
- 1 Firm avocado
- 1 Large tomato (not ripe)
- 1 Tender onion or a couple of shallots
- 1 Yellow pepper
- 1 Red pepper
- A bunch of cilantro

Vinaigrette:
- 2 tsp Dijon mustard
- 1 tbsp Honey
- Juice of one lime
- Olive oil & Jerez vinegar (3 parts oil with 1 vinegar)

To plate:
Voatsiperifery pepper if you have it,
otherwise any aromatic pepper.
Wasabi or fresh English Mustard.

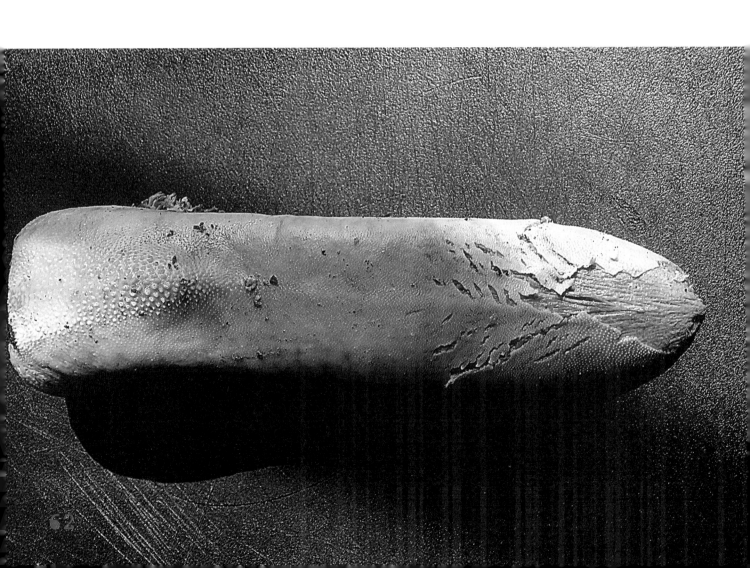

Rub whole tongue with a salty dry rub.
Vacuum seal and Sous Vide at 72°C for 48 hours.
Shock in iced water.
When fairly cool remove the skin and trim the tongue.
Either reseal in a vacuum or zipper bag or, ideally, press in a tongue press if you have one.
Before using rest in a freezer for 20 minutes. This will enable you to slice it more easily.

Coarsely chop the salad ingredients and mix by hand.
Whisk dressing together and mix with the salad in a large bowl.
Layer consecutive thin slices of tongue with the salad.
Coarsely grate Voatsiperifery pepper on top
Dot mustard on around side of plate.

As a bonus, once you've cooked your tongue, you can make 'Tacos de Lengua'. Toast a few corn tacos. On these stack a bit of pulled tongue, avocado, red onions, tomatoes and torn coriander. Give it a splash of hot Chipotle salsa, maybe Cholula, or make you own by blending a can of Chipotle peppers. Stick on a sombrero and do the hat dance. Cultural appropriation at its finest.

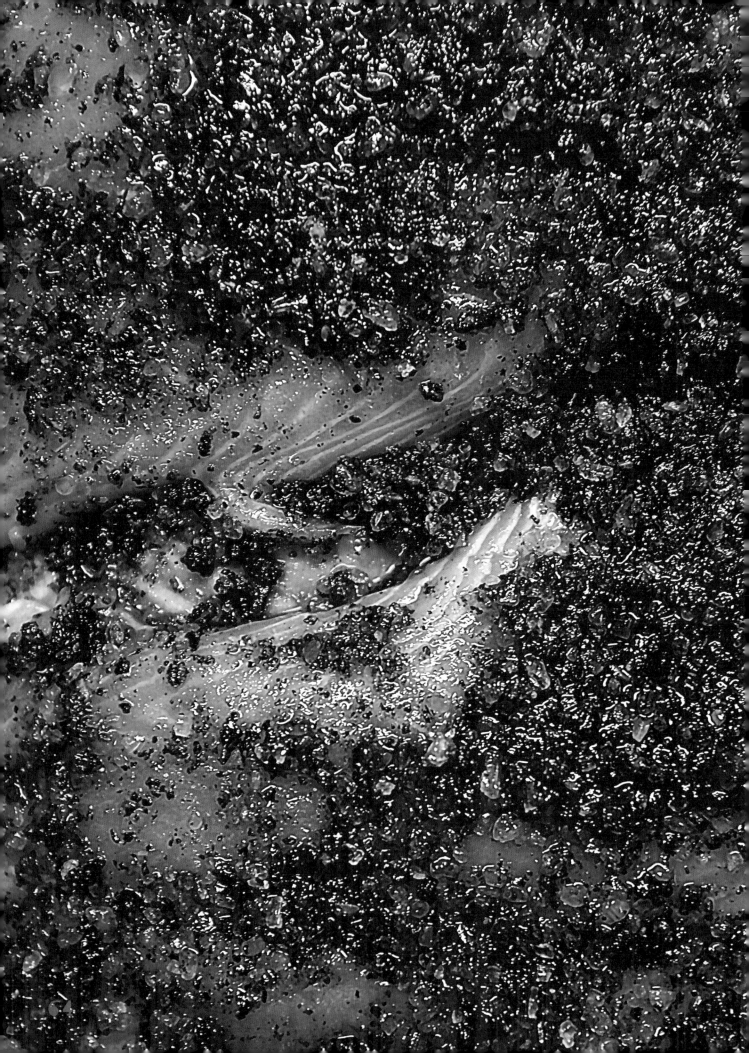

Salmon Negroni

I created this in Penang for a dinner party that was to feature cocktails.
I found fresh juniper berries in a tropical herb and butterfly garden; from there the rest transpired.
The salmon is cured in salt, sugar, gin and juniper berries then soaked in Vermouth. At the time I had to use that Italian muck, Martini Rosso, but since I have used a good Catalan Vermut. To complete the Negroni I accompanied it with a Campari sorbet though subsequently swapped this for the less bitter Aperol.

In the restaurant it became quite a signature dish and was hugely popular but is a piece of piss to make as long as you set the alarm and don't overdo it.

Whole fresh salmon, 2-3kg, filleted and pin-boned and a bottle of good Catalan Vermut

A word about pin-boning. It is not difficult but is essential. Get a small pair of long-nosed pliers, if possible with a curved tip. From the wide end run your thumb down the centre and pull them out.

Dry cure:
- Gin
- I cup Coarse salt
- I cup Caster sugar
- I cup Juniper berries
- I sprig Fresh chopped dill
- I tsp Zest of an unwaxed lemon

Method:
Grind the salt, sugar and juniper in a blender. .
Moisten mixture with the gin until like wet sand.

Line a baking tray with cling-film.
Heavily rub mixture all over the fish and press this firmly into the flesh. Bring up sides of the cling-film and wrap around. Leave in the fridge for 8/12 hours, certainly no more.

Rinse the mix from the salmon well under cold running water and pat dry. Lay out salmon in Tupperware then completely cover in Vermut. Leave in fridge for a minimum of 3 days but it will last much longer.
.
To plate slice finely at a diagonal across the width of the fish.
Serve with Aperol sorbet, possibly, a seaweed salad and a shot of Negroni on the side.

Ron Katz –
Rum Smoked Brisket & Pickle

Our tribute to the immortal Katz's Deli in New York. "I'll have what she's having"

Brisket, about 1.5kg, trimmed of outer fat

Injection mix:
- 1/3 cup Rum
- 1/3 cup Brown sugar
- 120 g Butter

Soften mix in a pan on a low heat, stirring constantly. Do not allow to get too hot. Allow to cool.

Wrap the brisket in cling film.
With a meat syringe inject the liquid through the film along the whole length. It will leak out. Don't worry. Just keep going. Seal with more film and put to one side in warm place.

Preheat a cold smoker to approximately 95-100°C . Hickory or Maple wood seems to work best here.

Remove any cling film from the rum-injected beef. Pat dry and place on a rack in the middle of the smoker. Smoke for 1 hour or until an instant thermometer reads 55°C.

Pat very dry then vacuum seal the meat. Sous Vide in a water bath at 56°C for 48 hours. If you are not going to use it, immediately shock the sealed bag in a bath of ice for 10 minutes then store it in the fridge.

When it comes to carving, pop it in the freezer for 30 minutes, You'll find it much easier to slice finely.

Russian dressing:

- 1 cup Mayonnaise
- ¼ cup Tomato ketchup
- 1 tsp Hot chipotle
- 1 tsp Worcestershire sauce
- ¼ tsp Sweet paprika
- ½ tsp Mustard powder
- Fine sea salt

Stir all the ingredients together.
Store in a squeezy sauce bottle.

To serve:

Pumpernickel bread
Dill pickles
Black garlic
Rocket

Take a slice of pumpernickel bread and cut in half lengthways.
Smear with Russian dressing.
Place a couple of leaves of rocket crossways so they hang out of the side.
Place thin slices of the brisket on top.
Top with dill pickle, sliced lengthways.
Finally a blob of dressing and a slither of black garlic.

Lightly sprinkle the edges of the plate with warm rum for the aroma. Serve with a shot of rum punch on the side.

Leg of Lamb stuffed with Crab

In my twenties I lived in a splendid Georgian house opposite Primrose Hill belonging to my godfather, Guy. We had the ground floor, Guy and his Belgian wife the upper floors and his curious son the basement. Guy was director of the family shoe store in Bond Street.

At the other end of Regent's Park Road he had bought a house for his long time mistress, Maudy, a racy ex showgirl. It was his custom every evening to announce that he was taking the dog for a walk. They had no dog. He would return a few hours later, slightly refreshed. Everyone was quite happy with this arrangement.

When the wife passed away he rightly proposed to his mistress. The wedding reception for his original marriage, a rather grand affair, had been held at the legendary Café Royal, just before the war.

First prepare the stuffing.

Personally, for most dishes, I prefer the dark crab meat but for this you will need a blend of both dark and white.

Mix the following:
• 500 g Fresh crab meat (if not use canned)
• 100 g Chopped fresh ginger
• Sprig of spring onions including the tops, finely chopped.
• Sprig of wild garlic, diced or 4 cloves of fresh garlic if not
• 2 stems Lemon grass
• 2 tbsp Lemon zest, finely diced
• A bunch of fresh Coriander, coarsely chopped
• 1 tsp Ground Sichuan pepper

He wanted a lesser reception with just four guests but recalled that the highlight of the original dinner was leg of Welsh lamb stuffed with crab meat, an innovative and extravagant dish for those times. He conferred with the current head chef who was intrigued and consulted their ancient archives, The chef found a record of that very dinner, complete with the recipe which he prepared and proudly presented to the wedding table.

Sadly I have no access to this tome but this is my tribute to that dish. I think that it worked out well.

So get yourself a leg of lamb (2/2.5Kg), not just any old one but, ideally, salt marsh lamb from either Romney Marsh or Gower. If not Waitrose will do.

In the thigh make a deep pocket and cram all the stuffing in to it. If possible, sew it up with butcher's twine.

20 minutes before cooking liberally cover the lamb with salt. Heat the oven to 200°C. When ready brush off the salt and smother with oil. Place in oven. After an hour check the internal temperature. You want about 55°C for nice pink meat.

Take it from the oven, open the crab pocket, remove the stuffing, and set aside. Cover the lamb with foil and rest for ten minutes or so. Meanwhile drain the juices and add a good slug of either Mirim or Pedro Ximénez and a dash of cooking soy. Thicken with cornflour.

Carve the lamb across the grain. Plate the meat, pour on a splash of gravy and top with a spoonful of stuffing. Serve with steamed Pak Choi and roast potatoes.

Almost worth getting married for!

CORONATION CHICKEN

Supposedly devised by Constance Spry for the coronation of the late Queen Elizabeth II, her recipe bears a remarkable resemblance to Jubilee Chicken made for the silver jubilee of George V in 1935. And if she can plunder history then so can I.

This is a rather more healthier version with Crème Fraîche and Greek Yogurt replacing the buckets of double cream in the Spry original though no less luscious for it.

Top it off with gold leaf if you want to go regal.
Gold is indigestible so you'll be poohing gold the next day on the throne.

Traditionally it is served with cold white rice but, in keeping with the health tip, I prefer a bit of fennel and orange salad.

4 happy chicken breasts.
Bunch of fresh coriander

Sauce:
• 100 g Apricots, pre-soaked overnight in Pedro Ximénez
• 80 g Toasted almonds
• 3 tbsp Curry powder, toasted on a hot pan
• 2 tbsp Ground Ginger
• 2 tsp Worcestershire Sauce
• 2 tbsp Apricot Jam
• 2 tsp Hot Lime Pickle

Blend all the above well then stir in:
200 ml Crème fraîche
200 ml Greek Yogurt

Vacuum seal the chicken breasts with salt, pepper and a pinch of curry powder.
Sous Vide at 66°C for 3 hours.
Shock with ice to cool.

Chop the cold chicken into small pieces about 1 cm square and mix with the sauce. Chill in the fridge for at least 4 hours, preferably overnight.

Just before you serve, mix finely chopped fresh coriander into it.

Portion the mixture with a steel ring onto each plate. Top with toasted almonds and a PX apricot.

Surround with green leaves of some sort and dust the edge with beetroot powder.

LANCASHIRE HOTPOT

Lancashire Hotpot is thought to have originated in the 19th century for the workers in the mills of the North. It could be put on at breakfast time to be ready for tea after work. It needs long slow cooking.

Some people reckon that you can use any old meat for a Lancashire hotpot but in my book it is strictly only neck of lamb, in fact not just lamb but old mutton. Luckily nowadays we have plenty of Muslim butchers around and they do like a bit of mutton. The flavour is stronger and, as the sheep are old, the cuts are larger. However use lamb or hogget if needs be.

As to the difference, it varies slightly from country to country but, roughly speaking, spring lamb is slaughtered at about 6 months old, hogget in its second season so it is between one and two years old. Mutton is the old bastard of the family.

Back in England I used to cycle to Borough Market on Saturdays. This was before it got hip and the prices had overtaken Harrods'. There was a butcher who used to drive his meat wagon down from Morecambe every weekend and I would buy neck of mutton each visit. I told him that my Ma hailed from there, He asked me what I did with it. He was delighted until I told him how I cooked it. As far as he was concerned hotpot had three ingredients and no more: Neck of mutton, onions and potatoes. Even salt he was a bit suspicious of, herbs were unnecessary and garlic was foreign muck and the devil's work. He was never quite the same after that discussion.

Anyway given here is my soft southern bastard version:

- 2 Necks of mutton sliced to 2 cm
- 500 g Lamb's kidneys, cut in half
- 3 Lamb's tails if you can find any
- 1 kg King Edward or Maris Piper potatoes
- 1 kg Large onions
- Fresh thyme and a few bay leaves
- 3 cloves of Satan's garlic, finely chopped
- An Oxo cube, crumbled
- A splash of Worcestershire sauce.
- A bottle of dry white wine

Peal the onions and, with a mandolin, slice, cut across to form whole discs, 4mm thick. Wash the potatoes and, without peeling, slice to 8mm.

Brown the lamb in batches in a very hot cast iron pan, a single layer at a time. Set aside. In the same pan deglaze the bottom with a small amount of wine then add the rest and reduce by a third, adding the Oxo cube and Worcestershire sauce.

Take a heavy casserole dish and butter the bottom and sides. Stick vertical slices of potato to the sides. Now, starting with potato, layer onions, meat and potato. On each meat layer add garlic, kidney, thyme and an occasional bay leaf. You want to finish with a potato layer on the top. Pour the reduced wine down the side until it reaches no more than half way up. Finally, if you have them, place the lamb tails across the top.

Fit a lid or cap of tin foil and put the dish in the oven at 150°C for 3 hours, after which remove the lid, up the temperature to 180°C and cook for 30 minutes or until the potatoes on top brown. Serve with greens.

Goes well with a decent Burgundy or chilled Beaujolais

CLAYPOT KUNG PAO FROG LEGS

Found all over Asia, and especially in the hawkers' markets of Singapore and Malaysia, the dish originates from Szechuan province in China. Frog Legs are most delicate and very healthy. You will find them, frozen, in Vietnamese stores. However if you are squeamish about the idea try the same sauce on cooked chicken.

For the salsa:
- 1 tbsp Light soya sauce
- 1 tbsp Kecap Manis (sweet soya sauce)
- 1 tbsp Corn flour
- 1 tbsp Oyster sauce
- 1 tbsp Sugar
- 1 tbsp Minced garlic
- 1 tbsp Minced ginger
- 5 to 8 fresh Red bird's eyes chillies
- 1 tbsp Szechuan peppercorns

Whisk all together in a pan and warm.

Take 3 sprigs spring onion, white parts chopped fine, green parts in 3 cm sections.

Put 6/8 frozen frog's legs in a zip lock bag.
Place in Sous Vide bath at 56°C for 7 minutes.

Remove frog legs and put on hot plancha for 30 seconds each side.
Add frog legs to the pan of salsa and stir

Decant all to a hot terracotta dish.

Dress with spring onions and serve with steamed green beans.

72hr Pork with Minty Mustard Peas

Great for a large party as all the work is done ahead.
The vacuum-sealed bags will keep in the fridge for weeks once cooked so make lots in one go.
Good for a rainy day or a lazy Sunday afternoon,

Cut an unsalted pork belly of about 3 or 4 kg into 250 g portions. Score diagonally both ways.
Rub pork belly with honey, paprika and salt. Vacuum seal each portion.
Submerge in water at 77°C for 10-20 seconds to kill any lactobacillus on the surface of the meat.

Sous Vide at 57°C for 48/72 hours.
When the time is up shock in iced water and refrigerate.

Peas:
Boil 2 bags of frozen peas.
Drain and rest until warm.
Add 125 ml Crème fraîche, a dollop of Dijon mustard and a large handful of torn mint leaves.
Liquidise with an immersion blender.

To serve, drop each bag of pork back in the water bath for 10 minutes. Remove from the bag, reserve the liquid and pat with kitchen roll until dry.

Griddle, skin side down, on a very hot plancha until crisp.
Slightly brown the other sides for a few seconds. Remove from the grill and slice into two down the middle.

Reheat peas.
Plate pork atop a ring of peas.
Dress with a mint leaf.
Smear with a blob of Dijon mustard.
For gravy just add the reserved liquid to Bisto and add a good slug of dry sherry.

Bourbon, Bacon & Chilli Jam

- 500 g of Bacon
- A couple of handfuls of finely chopped onion
- A whole bulb of smoked garlic, ditto
- 1 tsp Chilli powder:
- 1 Jalapeño pepper
- 1 tsp Smoked paprika
- 250 ml Bourbon
- 200 ml Date syrup - or Maple if none available
- A good slug of Balsamic Modena
- 1 tsp Brown sugar

Chop the bacon into small pieces and fry on medium heat until very crispy. Remove the bacon, leaving fat in the pan, and dry it on kitchen roll.

In the remaining bacon fat sauté onions and garlic until browning. Add spices and sweat for a while.

Pour in the bourbon and flame to remove alcohol. (NB *have a fitted lid for your pan ready to put out flames before the kitchen catches fire*)

Add syrup, vinegar and sugar and simmer really low for 20 minutes or so. Do not burn!

Allow to cool then decant to a mason jar.

Store in the fridge until you open the fridge door again and put it on whatever you are just about to eat.

Hide from the other members of the household. It should keep for weeks but it won't.

Hasselback Potato Gratin

- 2 kg Large potatoes
- 200 g Manchego curado cheese, finely grated
- 500 ml Cream
- A few cloves of chopped garlic
- 1 tbsp Fine herbs
- 1 Chicken stock-cube
- Tonka bean

Warm oven to 200°C
Slice potatoes about 4mm thick with a mandolin.
In a large bowl mix cream, cheese, garlic, herbs and a stock cube. Add potato, mixing well so all slices are completely covered.

Grease a deep baking tray and vertically rack up the potato slices in rows. Pour any cream mix remaining in the bowl over the potatoes. The liquid should come about halfway up the spuds. If not add some additional cream. Grate a little tonka bean on top.

Tightly cover the dish with tin foil and place it in the oven. After half-an-hour remove tin foil and return to the oven for at least another hour until the tops of the potatoes are very crisp.

For a variation of Jansson's Temptation, a classic Swedish dish, just add pickled sprats or boquerones as you are layering it up.

QUESO BORRACHO

This was originally inspired by Jonathan Meades' Rebarbe, ironically from his book 'The Plagiarist in the Kitchen'. where he had, in turn, stolen it from Philippe Regourd.

It was only when I had a go that I realised it was, essentially, a boozy Spanish version of English Potted Cheese.

To be served at the end of a meal.

If you're not already pissed enough at this stage in the proceedings, you will be after eating this but if you want to go the whole hog get out the Chateau d'Yquem 1986. We did and very fine it was too.

Failing that, just neck the rest of the Cardenal Mendoza. It's not going to hang around very long in any case.

- 500g Unpasteurised Cabrales cheese
- 100g Soft, unsalted butter
- 100 g Crème fraîche
- 250 ml Cardenal Mendoza brandy

Crumble the cheese and soften the butter then chuck everything in a blender and whoosh.
Scrape into a mason jar and leave in the fridge for a few days to let the flavours develop.
Serve with warm baguettes at the end of a meal.

MARROW RUM

I cobbled this recipe together from various sources many years ago. I have never got around to trying it, but it has to be done and you are the one. It possibly sounds quite lethal and I take no responsibility for your subsequent blindness if you choose so to do.

Wipe a very large ripe marrow clean with damp cloth, then saw a piece off the top end. Set this cap aside and scoop out all the seeds and pith with a long handled spoon.

Press demerara sugar into the cavity and fill it right up to the top. Pour in activated wine yeast, from home brew shops, and add the juice of an orange. Replace the end of the marrow and seal with gaffer tape. Suspend the marrow over a bowl and leave in a warm place.

After a couple of weeks unseal the end of the marrow and top up with more sugar. Some of the first lot should have been absorbed into the flesh of the marrow. Replace the cap again and reseal. At this point you may want to hang it in muslin before the whole lot collapses.

Leave for a few more weeks until the marrow starts to drip from the bottom into the bowl. All the sugar should have been absorbed by the flesh of the marrow. Spike a hole in the bottom and allow the liquid to drain into the bowl. Strain it into a fermentation jar and fit airlock.

Keep at least three months and up to a year. The longer you leave it, the stronger it will become.

If you have been brave enough to not just make it but drink some and still have your vision, please let me know and I will gladly buy you a very decent lunch for the opportunity to taste this hillbilly nectar.

CORIANDER AND WALNUT PESTO

- 2 Large bunches chopped coriander
- 2 Garlic cloves
- 1 Jalapeño pepper, seeded and chopped
- 1 cup Walnuts, toasted
- 1 Squirt of lemon juice
- 80 g Parmesan
- 200 ml Spicy olive oil
- A pinch of red pepper flakes

Coarsely chop the coriander.
Put ¾ of it in the blender with everything but the oil.
Very slowly dribble oil in while slowly running the blender.
Hand chop the rest of the coriander then stir in.
Salt and pepper to taste.
Add more oil to thin it out if desired.

JAPANESE PICKLED CUCUMBER

Slice cucumber longways on Mandolin
Heavily salt in a bowl for 30/40 minutes then rinse

- 200 ml Chinese or Sushi Vinegar
- 2 tbsp Sugar
- Slug of sesame oil
- Good slug sweet soy
- 1 tbsp Minced fresh ginger

Mix above until sugar dissolves

Add a good pinch of dried daikon to cucumber and put in a mason jar.
Poor vinegar mix over and top up with more vinegar to cover.
Ready in an hour or so. Keeps for a week or two.

Tartar Sauce

- 1 cup Hellmann's mayonnaise
- 2 Dill pickles, chopped very small
- 2 tbsp Fresh lemon juice
- 2 tbsp Capers, chopped
- 2 tbsp Chopped fresh dill
- 1 tsp Worcestershire sauce
- 1 tsp Dijon mustard
- Salt and pepper

Stir it all gently together and decant.

Tomato Butter

- 2 cups Cherry tomatoes
- 1 tsp Thyme leaves
- 250 g Warm unsalted butter
- Freshly ground black pepper
- ½ tsp Salt flakes

Grill tomatoes then blend everything.
Chill, man!

STRANGER &

STRANGER

CALÇOTS & CALÇOTADES

There are few foods that are accompanied by protective clothing. Eating the banned Sardinian sheep cheese, Casu Marzu, you are advised to wear safety goggles to prevent the flies from the maggots that inhabit this festering pecorino leaping into your eyes. There is no such danger in consuming calçots but it can get very messy, so you are supplied with both bib and gloves to protect your clothes and your decorum.

I would not go so far as to say delicacy but Calçots are a Catalan delight from Valls and have EU PGI status. Green onions are planted in trenches and, as they reach for the sky, more earth is heaped on them, causing what would otherwise be a round onion to elongate to more like an oversized spring onion or leek.

Traditionally they are eaten in large groups at a macia, a farmhouse restaurant in the countryside. These events are known as calçotades. The calçots are cooked outside in huge batches on open  wood fires until they are thoroughly charred all over then wrapped in newspaper. This is part of the cooking process as they are tenderised by the steam created within.

Served at long communal tables, a bunch at a time, on brick tiles with Romesco sauce on the side, this is where it gets very messy. After putting on your PPE you take a hot calçot by the end, grab the charred outer skin and firmly tug along the shaft, as if you were removing a large black condom. Now green and moist the Calçot is dunked in the red salsa until dripping, then dangled over your wide open mouth gaping skywards like a 5 day old chick, lowering the calçot vertically down. Probably not ideal for a first date though it can be quite sensual once all dignity is abandoned. So like most casual sex really then.

Each person consumes up to a dozen, washed down with cold red wine from a porrón, those pointy nosed decanters, passed around the table as tradition dictates. Plates of mixed meat follow, including morcilla and chorizo, cooked over the embers of the wood fire. The meal is finished off with Crema Catalana, coffee and shots of disgusting spirit, Orujo, better suited to filling a Zippo.

SNIPS AND SNAILS AND PUPPY DOG TAILS

I've always boasted that I'd eat anything that didn't involve a bet
A. A. Gill

Asia is home to what , to most westerner's sensibilities, is the plain disgusting. One man's exotic delicacy is another woman's UGH! This is a matter of personal preference, taste, morality and ethics. So it is Eastwards that this intrepid gourmet must head. It is said that you can eat all mushrooms but some only once. I 'll generally give anything a go as long as someone else has tried it first and lived. I would be inclined to add that it was already dead but then a fresh oyster is a think of beauty and should still be alive.

Donghuamen Night Market, just off Tinammen Square, is the Borough Market of creepy crawlies. The sort of things you would stamp on, not stick them in your mouth. Others you are amazed how it is possible to eat them.

Among the bug department we have Water Beetles, Longhorn Beetles, Centipede, Bee Cocoon, Silk Worms, Bamboo Worms, Tarantula, Locusts and just the unidentifiable. It is a long way to come just to go for a Burger King so I worked my way through the lot, crunch after crunch. The insects seemed to divide into two basic categories: Crunchy things and slimy things with lots of legs, right up to millipedes, or the slimy without any legs although one does suspect that something may hatch out the latter. All had one mutual trait: absolute lack of any flavour. I was baffled why anybody would choose to eat them.

食品名称	单位	单价 人民币/元	食品名称	单位	单价 人民币/元
炸羊鞭、炸海蛇 Sheep penis/Sea snake	串	50	金边龙虱、炸蜈蚣、海星 Water beetel/Centipede/Bean worm/Starfish	串/个	30/20
鱿鱼头、金枪鱼 Sleeve-fish head/Tunny	串	10	(养殖) 鲨鱼、蜂蛹 Baby shark/Bee cocoon/Bamboo worm	条/串	40/15
鸡心、鸡肉、鸡胗、炸臭豆腐 Chicken heart/ Chicken/Stinking dou fu	串	5	皮皮虾、小龙虾、大虾 PiPi prawn/Fried-crayfish/Fried-prawns	串	15
羊肉串、炸蚕蛹 Lamb/Dog/Silk-worm	串	5	墨鱼、海胆、海菇 Fried cuttle fish/ Sea urchin/Sea-mushroom	串	15

The offerings are not just limited to bugs. Sea food gets in on the act. Sea Horses, while technically a fish, are not only crunchy but are rather sharp and could well slice your gullet on the way down, I was intrigued how the Starfish were to be eaten, They are deep fried then a small flap on the underside is lifted and some inner goo spooned out and was almost edible. I have had it at Noma in Copenhagen and it was no better or worse.

Not everything was too unpleasant. Sea Urchins are divine in any context although Beijing is a long way from the sea. Baby shark is, well, shark but not my favourite fish. I certainly wasn't going to eat dog. Not Dogfish, this was deep fried Fido, and not just the tail. That was not going on my plate, ever. However in Sheep's Penis I found something I would return for. Looking like a meaty Curly Wurly I had finally got myself some Beijing Cock and was keen for more.

Initially I had assumed that the market was just a tourist attraction so the locals could point and laugh at 'big nose', as Westerners are known, tucking in to the indigestible. But it was clear that 'bridge and tunnel' Chinese came up on a Saturday night especially to dine out on what they genuinely consider to be gastronomic treats.
Bloody sight cheaper than Borough Market too.

It's alive

There are hurdles, though, which challenge even this intrepid explorer. In Beijing, on a whim, my pal Tim and I thought we would try a new Japanese restaurant in the World Trade Centre. Central to the room was a large chest high tank full of fish. At the far end of this was the chef's station, the other sides forming a bar around which patrons sat,

Not understanding the language we ordered a set menu which clearly included Nemo swimming in front of us. We had got through a few tasty morsels when the chef at the end gave us a wave, got out a net and went fishing. Moments later what appeared to be a whole fish, encased in a pyramid of ice, arrived and lay pointing at Tim opposite me.

'It's staring at me' he said.

He revolved the plate and, sure enough, it was not only swivelling its eyes, now in my direction, but gasping for air. Welcome to "The Living Fish", a much lauded Japanese delicacy, lying there ready to watch you eat its own flesh delicately carved from its body into sashimi and surrounding it. I turned it back to Tim. I didn't want it memorising my face so it could hunt me down in the afterlife.

Now this was a certain moral dilemma for the traveling gourmet. Its fate was already sealed though. I justified that it would have been an insult to let it die in vain and an insult to the proud chef. Pathetic, I know but it was very tasty.

The next day Tim mentioned this to his Chinese secretary. She was familiar with it. Her Japanese boyfriend was a fan but, just to rub salt in the wound, put Wasabi mustard in its mouth to watch it thrash about.

No wonder, I thought, that there is a Museum of Japanese Atrocities just a few blocks from where we had sat.

However I later learnt that the Chinese have a similarly dubious dish, involving holding the fishes' head in a cloth and dunking the rest of its body in boiling oil while still conscious.

'"Nowt so queer as folk" my Pa would have said.

THE BIG STINK

There are some foods that are foremost defined by their possibly nauseous aroma though once you get past the nasal assault these can potentially be very rewarding. However be warned, if any of these are to be savoured do not try in your own home. I once cooked a rather gamy jugged hare in its own blood. It was magnificent but the apartment was haunted by the beast for a couple of months afterwards. The poor owner had all the windows open through a bitter winter and still it lingered.

No smoking

No eating or drinking

Fine $1000   Fine $500

No flammable goods

No durians

Fine $5000

DURIAN

Throughout the Singapore metro system it is forbidden to carry durian and quite rightly too. Anyone who has wandered along Gerrard Street in China Town during the summer would be familiar, though not necessarily recognise, the wafts of warm sweet baby sick with back notes of spice. They might notice the prickly melon size fruit on the market stalls and wonder. If one can overcome the initial dread, the taste of this fruit is luscious and, oddly, once tried, the odour becomes less nappy-like and starts to make sense. Now it is your own child's output and that is OK. Own it. Nobody wants to smell others farts but your own are quite acceptable. Just don't bring them back home. The custard like pulp from this fetid fruit takes over and you will never be haunted by the aroma again. In Singapore I immediately seek out Durian ice cream, an acceptable introduction without the reminders of bringing up baby. I have always wanted to try it in a savoury curry, just not in my house.

SURSTRÖMMING

I suspect that it could be something to do with the long summer days or bleak winters but the Scandinavians just love their putrid fish. In Norway they have Rakfisk made from trout and is relatively mild. In Iceland they make Hákarl by burying Greenland shark in the sand for 2 or 3 months. Unfortunately they then dig it up and, god forbid, eat it.

Not to be outdone the Swedes produce Surströmming, herrings that are picked in brine then allowed to ferment all to a strict timetable. Caught during April & May the fish is brined and stored in open barrels until July when it is canned. Here it continues to ferment and fester. Finally, from the third Thursday of August, "Surströmming day" the tins are opened to much jubilation. Probably not the best of days to go to the Stockholm food market.

It is difficult to describe without invoking old ladies piss soaked gussets. Once you have cracked open the can, it is impossible to believe that this is considered edible. Some recommend opening it undersea which has to be better than not. You then have the opportunity to just empty the contents out and return these poor dead fish corpses to whence they came,

But someone has to try so you don't have to. I took one for the team. I would love to say that, once you got over the stink of a Glastonbury pissoir it had its rewards but, once I stopped gagging, it was unable to say much at all. Luckily I had armed myself with a bottle of Linie from Norway. One of the finest Aquavits produced it travels around the world for a year, crossing the equator twice. I wasn't waiting that long, I wasn't even getting it in a glass, necking straight from the bottle to sluice the disgusting flesh down between gags.

I was told that it is an acquired taste but I cannot imagine how anyone would continue eating it so as to do so. It used to be sold in Stockholm airport but since all the major airlines banned it 20 years ago it is harder to find. I think the world is better off left that way.

EAT ART

Whenever I create a photographic show or event I try to involve food in some way. Different examples of this were at the opening of my exhibition at the appropriately named Eat Meat gallery in Barcelona.

For any edible printing you need a dedicated new printer. You cannot have traces of potentially poisonous chemicals from ordinary ink. Luckily companies virtually give A4 home printers away as they make most of their profits from the ink. You just need to make sure you can buy cartridges pre-filled with edible inks or fillable empty cartridges for the appropriate printer. Canon and Epson seem to be popular.

To get started:
Bakers started the trend so you can get printable icing sheets but for our purpose we use rice or wafer papers. You can even get 'coffee toppers' to float on your foamy beverage. Try these on an egg-based cocktail or a draft stout with a good head.

Homage to
[kətəlúnə]

A MASS PORTRAIT EVENT BY OLIMAX. NOV 26TH. FROM 12 PM UNTIL 8 PM

EAT MEAT

lefreak

G&T Jelly Portraits

For the Barcelona show we made G&T Jellies with portraits from the show embedded within.

It was curious to see the subjects eating themselves so to speak.

Print your subjects on A4, each no larger than 4cm then cut out. Use a juniper forward gin like Beefeater or Tanquery.

First add gelatin to a small amount of water and allow to bloom. Use 50% more than recommended for total liquid as you want it fairly stiff. If you want it vegetarian substitute agar for the gelatin ... or just don't tell anyone

You want to work on ratio of 1:1 gin and water. Stir in the gelatin adding a teaspoon of citric acid and a dash of liquid stevia for each 500cl. Pour into a baking tray to a depth of 1cm. Keep level while it sets in the fridge overnight.

With a Stanley knife cut in half for top and bottom. Lay your individual edible rice paper prints in neat rows on the bottom half to form a grid with spacing of 2cm or so then cut out each jelly. Leave them out at room temperature for a short while so the halves will stick together then return to the fridge.

Pork Prints

Using the same kit much larger prints can be made on whole joints of meat for instance. After a bit of trial and error we've found that pork belly works well. Make a print up to A4 on Wafer or Rice paper. You may need a few as, if it is not quite right, you need to quickly whip it off and try with a new one.

Roast your joint and, while the skin is slightly warm, carefully lower the paper onto the skin. It is a bit like dealing with sheets of gold at this stage, the prints almost being sucked into position. Looks great when you're done though. Better than a wedding cake.

PICA PICA, INNIT

British pubs have long had 'tapas' of sorts, they just didn't have a collective name for it. Pickled eggs, pickled onions, pork pies, scotch eggs, pints of cockles or whelks, pork scratchings, and other bar snacks ideal for sharing sat along the counter to wash down with your generally insipid ale.

When I did an exhibition of Barcelona at Eat Meat gallery I though it would be amusing to do some British finger food for the opening, tongue firmly in cheek. It worked out rather well; in the end the Catalans loved it. Here are a couple of examples of those we did.

KEDGEREE NORI

Coarsely chop 3 hard boiled eggs

Rinse 300g basmati rice until water runs clear then soak for 30 minutes and drain well.

Slowly fry up 4 diced shallots until transparent then add 2 tbsp good curry powder and 1 tsp turmeric and continue for a mo to toast the spices. Stir in rice and take off the heat.

Put 300 g of smoked haddock in a wide shallow pan with 2 bay leaves, barely cover with milk and simmer for 10 minutes.

Remove skin and flake the fish. Sieve the milk and add water to make up to 600ml

Put rice in a rice cooker along with the milk/water and switch on.

When ready gently combine by hand the cooked rice, flaked haddock, chopped eggs and half a bunch of shredded fresh coriander leaves. Add salt to taste. Do NOT add peas! They belong elsewhere.

While mixture is still warm lay out nori sheets, ladle a generous amount of rice at one end and slowly roll up like making a big fat reefer. The warmth from the rice should soften the seaweed as you go but if not steam over a kettle spout first.

Cut into 3 cm lengths. Serve while warm.

ROAST BEEF AND YORKSHIRES

If you are adventurous make, or otherwise buy, miniature Yorkshire puddings. Sous vide a fillet of brisket for a long time so it is rare but tender. When you are ready to serve put in freezer for 30 minutes first as it will be easier to carve thin slices.

Mix horseradish sauce with Crème fraîche. Put a teaspoonful of the mix in a warm Yorkshire pud, and add a rolled up slice of beef. Secure with a toothpick if needed.

FULL ENGLISH TAPAS

Hard boil some quail eggs

Fry a few cheap sausages the cut into rings. I say cheap as they have more breadcrumbs so more likely to hold together

Chop streaky bacon into 23cm lengths then fry until crispy.

In same pan toast cherry tomatoes until slightly charred and tiny button mushrooms

Now take long wooden cocktail stick and stick into a sausage ring. This is the base.

Now stack up, through the stick, a mushroom, bacon, quail's egg and tomato.

Cap with a single baked bean.

Optionally add Black pudding at the base end

If possible plate as a tower, the stick pointing towards heaven.

ETON MESS

Chop up a pound of strawberries and sprinkle with sugar and a good slug of Madeira.

Leave to macerate for half an hour. Whip a pint of whipping cream.

Crumble in four meringue nests. Gently fold in the fruit mixture.

Serve in glasses garnished with a couple of coriander leaves or churn in an ice cream maker for half on hour.

AND A PAIRING

El Celler de Can Roca

I have dined, actually mostly lunched, in some of the world's finest but there was one name, until recently, that somehow eschewed me. I could say that it was at the top of my bucket list but that cliché always reminds me, especially in the context of restaurants, of Monty Python's The Meaning of Life.

Maître d': "Ah, good afternoon, sir, and how are we today?"

Mr. Creosote: "Better."

Maître d': "Better?"

Mr. Creosote: "Better get a bucket, I'm going to throw up."

There was certainly no need for the bucket here but my mighty girth leapt in anticipation when I was invited to dine at El Celler de Can Roca in Girona. This legendary restaurant had been placed in the top three of the 'Worlds Best Restaurants' for a decade, topping the awards twice, before being fairly taken out of the running to sit amongst the Best of the Best. It was the last mountain I had to climb and I was heading for the summit.

Very much a family affair, the Celler is run by the three Roca brothers. Joan, is head chef, Josep the sommelier and Jordi, the youngest, the pastry chef. They grew up in their parents' modest restaurant, Can Roca, There, in 1986, they started their own place in an adjoining building, relocating to the current venue 20 years later. The year after they were awarded their third Michelin star.

Mama & Papa's original place is still there, just up the hill, but now with the addition of the brothers' more formal old extension. I've been there a couple of times. Any weekday you can get a three course Menu del Dia of classic Catalan fare for about 15 euros with wine included and very decent it is too. You can eat in either half though I feel more at home with the old boys in the original. It's where the food and family belong.

It is this family relationship and their upbringing within hospitality that is the backbone of what makes Celler de Can Roca so endearing. Their dedication and professionalism is unquestionable here but underlying this is a warmth that you don't often find at this standard of dining. Many three star restaurants can be soulless, a temple where you are expected to worship at the pass. Yet for all its fame Can Roca has somewhat the qualities of your local family-run trattoria or rather bodega. On any night at least one brother is present, though we were lucky to meet all three, and you get the impression that they would rather not be anywhere else. This is their home and they have invited you in. They greet all the guests, warmly, seemingly honoured that you have come to them not, as with some celebrity chefs, the other way around. It was clear that some guests were regulars, possibly locals, just as I wish I was, yet nobody was treated with indifference.

At the same time these boys do not rest on their laurels; at times they are hands on, whites on or sleeves rolled up in the kitchen and at the pass, getting down with their team. It is their personal reputation that is coming out from there and it is never going to be anything less that perfect. Joan has an open plan office right next to the kitchen so he can see what is going on at all times. You get the feeling that he is first in, last out, every day.

The room itself compliments this intimacy. It seats about 50 but is divided up so your table is only ever one of a pair. In the centre lives a glassed in miniature forest of young plane trees, mirroring the neighbouring parks of Girona where these trees line the wide avenues and are exported to Barcelona and beyond. Upon each table sit three stones to represent the three brothers lest you forget.

And so to the food. Isn't this what we came for? Well not exactly but let's see.
Our charming waiter, Andrea, brings what is the menu as such, a massive detailed list of courses but the choice is simple. The long one or the even longer one. Guess who won?
I am yet again reminded of Mr Creosote: "I'll have the lot"
Andrea's response is on script. " A wise choice."

The next choice is again binary: to wine flight or not, I am rarely keen on this idea but after a short debate luckily sanity prevailed and a wise choice it was too. When you have one third of the ruling family, sommelier Josep, entirely responsible just for the wines it is going to be outstanding and this turned out to be the case, possibly, without underplaying the food, the highlight of the evening.

Can Roca has a cellar of about 50,00 bottles, quite modest when you consider that they get through about 22, 000 a year. Located in the basement it takes up, naturally, one third of the available floorspace. Remarkably they have built a factory opposite, Roca Recicla, that recycles the empties into glassware and the like.

We were given a list of wines as we were leaving. I think we had about 20 different tastes, modest in volume but not in length. More often than not a new one was presented before I had a chance to finish the previous one which was good going for an alcoholic like me. For the long stretch of the multiple amuse-bouche we were generously supplied with Albet i Noya Brut Cava. After that it got silly!

The highlight for me was a Jerez that they had laid down in 1986, exclusively for the restaurant, the year that the brothers had started. There have only ever been 60 bottles. One recently went at a charity wine auction for over 5K euros. We were, reasonably, only given a thimbleful but I brutally held on to my glass, deigning just to give it the occasional sniff for 30 minutes. I have now drunk with the gods and they are up for it.

Not all wines were so extravagant but all, individually, had been carefully considered for their quality and relevance to the food that they would accompany. I would readily return just for the wine if I thought it possible.

I estimate that, in the end, we used 60 glasses between the 3 of us over the course of 20 odd wines, each glass different but of a shape appropriate to the style of wine. Glad I wasn't washing up although if I could work here, if only for a day, I'd scrub the loo floors. Someone must.

After Ferran Adrià, the brothers are considered some of the godfathers of contemporary Catalan cuisine. Partly responsible for the development of Molecular Gastronomy, Joan worked alongside the legendary culinary chemist, Hervé This, who coined the term.

The amuse-bouche, a few at a time, were explained in detail, without pretension, by Andrea including the year of creation. Here was a brief history of Can Roca in twelve tiny taste-bombs, each a explosion of joy to the palette, each one bringing its own individuality while complimenting its partners, though there was a dominance of truffle throughout. Not the chemical taste of truffle oil used by chefs on every bowl of squash soup the world over. These were undoubtedly fresh winter black truffles to be found buried beneath the base of oak trees, hunted by dogs or pigs around the forests of Catalonia in the first few months of the year. Just the aroma of truffles can take the lowliest item to new heights though an oyster here did seem lost beneath it.

The first five main courses were a remarkable demonstration that fine dining doesn't necessarily need fish, foul nor flesh to create deep, complex flavours, although the ingredients of some outnumbered many a whole menu elsewhere. Peas, steamed at the table in a wine of Xarel·lo, Catalonia's dominant native grape, with which it was served, led the way.

Calçots, Catalonia's unique forced onion, with razor clams smoothed the transition to the seafood dishes. A change of gear on the wine front to red heralded first game, by way of partridge, then "Remats de Foc", lamb three ways. Albert returned to carve their signature Poularde Brioche at the table.

While each dish throughout is presented in an individual way with custom-made place settings and tableware Can Roca utilises far less showmanship in the dining room than some other restaurants of this fame. I am sure they consider, quite rightly, that the quality of the fare can speak for itself. The grand theatrics are left to the last in the deserts with the Zen-like "It Rains in the Forest", another tribute to the local parks perhaps. A cloud of bubbles, spewing forth from a spout, is gathered up by Andea, and tossed in the air to be hung above a steel bowl where it rains down on the rest of the dish. Not half as spectacular as Heston Blumenthal's liquid nitrogen Ice cream machine but a clever piece of theatre nonetheless.

As a finale, in a tribute to the traditional dessert trolleys of grand hotel restaurants of yesteryear, a cart is wheeled up, laden with chocolate treats, though looking more like old-fashioned seaside ice cream stall. These playfull touches are likely to be from Jordi, the youngest of the brothers, whose province is pastry and sweets, the Willy Wonka of the family.

With these the sommelier dispenses a Mosel Riesling from Joh. Jos. Prüm, and Oremus Tokaji Aszú 3 Puttonyos 2016 (why not the 5 point, you may ask, but who would question the judgement of one of the world's greatest sommeliers)

For the last few years Can Roca, in particular Josep, has been distilling their own booze and making their own liquors under the Esperit Roca name. Their own Vermut de Carxofa (artichoke) had already been served with the artichoke rosette. To round off the desserts and, in fact the dinner, they presented Esperit Roca Licor de Cacau. It was complex and luscious without being overbearing. Dani immediately ordered the last three bottles in stock to take home. Who wouldn't?

In the end what, or rather who, makes this place so outstanding, so at the top of the game, is the collaboration of the brothers, their clear understanding of what fine dining really means and their obvious love of the game. The word is hospitality, that is what they grew up with, that is what they understand best, that is what they do better that anyone else in the world. It is, simply, put the World's Best Restaurant.

As we left Josep was waiting at reception and graciously thanked us for coming.
"I do hope to see you again soon"
I do hope so too, Josep.

El Cellar de Can Roca
Carrer de Can Sunyer, 48, 17007 Girona
www.cellercanroca.com

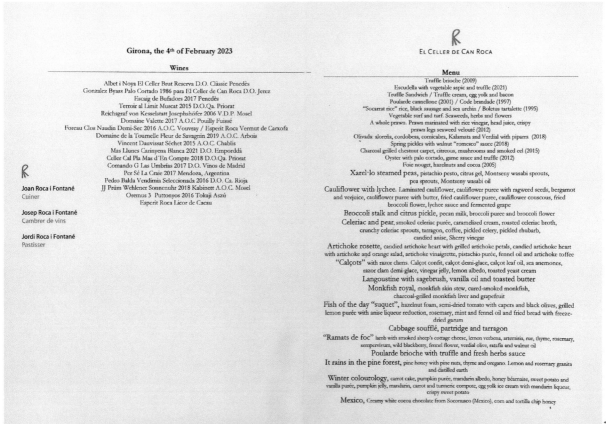

The Emperor's New Nordic

Whatever your profession there is always a pilgrimage lurking in the distance, a remote place that, one day, you aspire to venture to but that seems unobtainable. Suddenly, out of the blue, you get the call. There is a table for you at Noma next week. Can you confirm by this afternoon? This is a place that gets fully booked in hours when, three times a year, they open bookings for the coming season for a day. Fuck yeah.

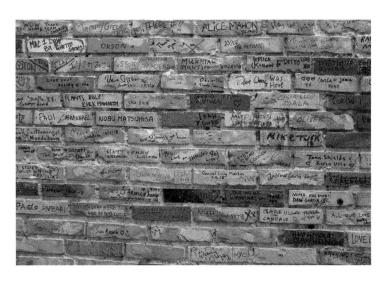

Noma, in its various incarnations, has been rated the world's best restaurant several times running. It is spoken of in hushed tones as a mythical beast. Does it still exist? Where is it now located? What happened in Mexico? Opened twenty years ago in Copenhagen by René Redzepi, it focuses on foraged leaves, fresh locally sourced produce (don't they all now?), the rare, the unusual, the obscure. A few years ago they shut up shop and took off for Mexico. I guess those Nordic nights get to you after a while. There have been other excursions to Australia and Japan. But now they were back in a new, purpose built venue on the outskirts of Copenhagen and our table awaited us.

Noma revolves around three seasons, Vegetable, Seafood and Game. Each is a surprise menu, together with a fixed wine pairing, for a set price of about 800 euros. There is no wine list, just take it or leave it. We were going in the seafood season so I had to prepare myself.

Due to an unfortunately incident at a well known Soho establishment I had become allergic to oysters about 30 years ago. At the time I didn't realise this was to be a permanent state and it took several rather messy incidents, often drunk, late at night, in Oyster bars, before my condition sunk in. I had learnt it is possible that the bacteria that lives on in your gut, like the Alien, eventually may leave you, though hopefully not through your chest like John Hurt. I hadn't had one for at least a decade or more so when asked if I had any allergies it was time to find out.

El Hogar Gallego is a very fine seafood restaurant in Calella, with tanks of live marine life, fresh oysters floating in trays atop. It is about 5 minutes from my then home. I had a fine dinner, at the end of which I ordered a coffee, a glass of sherry for courage, and one large raw oyster, all to be brought to the garden. I paid the bill and wandered outside. After sipping down the sherry, I shot the coffee back and, in one swift gulp, barely touching the sides, necked the oyster, and, without pause, rapidly legged it home where I sat on the pan, a previously prepared bucket for the front end (yes it is double-barrelled when it comes) and prayed. Then ... nothing. No violent explosion, no monster ripping though my

chest. The beast had left the building. I was cured and ready for anything that Noma might throw at me.

Not quite what Denmark in February could though. Living in a warm climate I have long abandoned coats, just leaving a couple in the UK, so I just threw on my heaviest tweeds and headed over. The first afternoon it was requested that we went to see the famous mermaid. This ugly amphibian midget lives out on the estuary where gale force winds fought their way up my trouser legs and swiftly removed all but a hint of the manhood I was certain I had tucked in that morning. Swiftly retiring back to the hotel I attempted its revival with a hot blow-job from the bathroom hair-dryer. Not an auspicious start.

So off to Noma. Considering its fame it took three taxis before one had even heard of it. He took us to their old location and had to be redirected out of town through farmland until we were dropped by the waterfront, next to a well lit, luckily heated, greenhouse. We were checked in and given a shot of much appreciated schnapps. This turned out to be a staging post holding a few other guests. One at a time we were called and led along the side of the main building that we then realised was the restaurant. We were let in through barn-like doors where we were individually welcomed by a 30 strong chorus of chefs. Charming in its way, I suppose, but it seemed quite pretentious and a rather inconsiderate use of the interns who, I gathered, came from all over the world to serve at the master's beckoning, for little or no pay. If you can spare them as greeters you have too many. They should be in front of a stove-top. We were led to our table but the same chant, repeated for each guest's arrival, got a bit tiresome, even from afar. This affectation was a precursor to the whole dining experience.

The restaurant, in this incarnation, was opened in 2018, a bespoke build by Danish architects the Bjarke Ingels Group. Set in the outskirts of Copenhagen's hippy enclave Christiania, on the water's edge between two lakes, it surrounds the main dining area with smaller outbuildings, all set in gardens where the chefs can cultivate seasonal ingredients. There is no doubting that it is of Nordic design and beautiful for it. High arched barn-like ceilings and huge windows looking onto the waterfront illuminate the bare wood tables and chairs. Opening onto this is an open-plan kitchen or rather the prep station. The overall effect is delightful, smart yet homely and warm, as are the staff, all of whom are charming though you don't get to know them very well as a different member attends the table each time. I suppose that when you have 100 staff to 40 covers everyone has to have a go but it adds to a rather impersonal atmosphere.

...... no, no, Noma, no more ...

And so to the menu.

You are kept to a strict timetable. Given every table is being served the same fare, it is more like a wedding service than gourmet dining: corporate function room catering with pretensions. At least there are no speeches.

However each dish arrives with a lengthy description about the item's heritage and which obscure leaf constitutes the blob of oil on it. Crucially which bit is edible as many of the bespoke bowls are so heaped with undergrowth, seaweed and other garnish that the tiny morsel of whatever is often barely discernible. I was often tempted to grab a handful of seaweed just to fill my mouth. I love seaweed, my salad of choice. Why could I not enjoy it? Is it not fresh? Instructions are given just how it should be eaten, though mostly this is just 'pick it up with your fingers'. I do know how to eat a bloody scallop, whatever weird jus had been splashed on it.

One does not go for a long gastronomic tasting menu of more than a dozen courses then complain that portions are too small. People who do are the sort that think a posh night out is going to Pizza Express rather than their usual Pizza Hut. It is entirely missing the point but in this case the idea of a tasting menu was a sham. What we have here is a shellfish course, some offcuts of cod then bits of a personalised crab, broken up and pretentiously served as individual courses. The skill of the kitchen is never in question. This is high end gastronomic cuisine; if only it tasted like it was.

The first few courses were individual shellfish. Pleasant enough, all with a similar citric edge and undertones of umami which was the ongoing theme. However one clam is not a course. There was even the shell of a reconstructed shrimp, only one each mind, that had been stuffed with a couple of edible flowers. These molluscs could all have been presented as one dish, saving the staff's shoe leather and us the wait between.

Next few 'dishes' were all various weird parts of a cod. Cod's tongue, still attached to the jaw bone like a Neanderthal lollipop, Cod's throat I think, then Cod 's bladder. I am all for trying the weird and wonderful but I now know that there is a reason not to eat the piss bag from a cod or any other fish, however much you mask it with obscure foraged herbs and fermented tea leaves. It tasted unpleasant as a good few other dishes did. I wondered if, given that they have 100 staff; did any one of them actually taste it and think 'Yum Yum, what a fabulous treat for my palate'. In the end it is just dinner and, especially at these prices, that is the minimum reaction to expect. The skin even appeared later, set in chocolate, for dessert. But what happened to the rest of the fish. The edible bit. Does that go for the staff dinner? If so I want in.

It was then the turn of the Atlantic King Crab, or rather, again, bits of one, mostly shell, strung out over a few more courses. This was not just any old crab though; it had its own calling card, I kid you not. We were each given a printed QR code so we could look up the name of our chap and leave a note of bereavement for its family. I wondered that, as we were each given one claw tip we could send them the other for a suitable burial in the family plot.

One introduction was given as "it has no meat in there but it has all that umami note from the fermentation itself". Could it not have included the meat itself? Would it not have not heightened the experience? Fermentation is a great part of the Noma philosophy. They published a large tome on the subject. I bought the book, They have a specialist facility and a master chef with his own lab within the complex. I don't have the patience for it. Some of Noma's pickles ferment for a couple of years. I suppose that if you have invested two years in the process then you are going to add it to the menu somewhere rather than assign it to the bin. It returns to the fundamental question: Does it taste nice?

Which takes us to the wines.

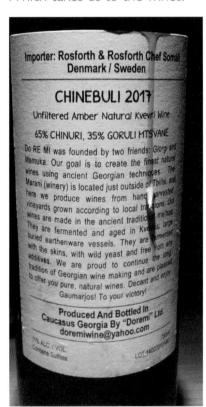

For some time I have been a great advocate of natural wines, those that have been grown with minimal intervention and, importantly, have no added sulphites. Sulphites occur naturally in all wine but viticulturists have been adding more since the Romans as a way of preserving the wine. Without this it is much harder to keep bacteria from spoiling it and this is where it can go horribly wrong. Natural wines do have reputation for having an unpleasant nose, somewhere between a wet Labrador and a compost heap. However not all of them do, it just takes more care.

In Noma there is no choice of wine. You pay 150 for the wine-flight and take what you are given All of them are natural but, sadly, many of them are unpalatable. I would have to say that, to be fair, they were, at least, very generous but that is like getting a bonus track on a Yoko Ono album.

At one point Cadman told the sommelier:
"This wine tastes like piss from a horse that has been declared unfit for work".
To his credit the chap took it in good humour. It was, after all, a pretty fair assessment.

Despite the insane cost of the menu, at the end they add 10% service. I wonder how much goes to the interns. For this 70 euros a head, I could get an outstanding lunch with a decent bottle in some of even London's finest, far more so in Barcelona.

Inevitably I must compare Noma with my favourite restaurant, Disfrutar, where you are served 30 courses of the most wonderful delights. Each one is very different, tiny morsels for sure and very theatrical in presentation, but each with a purpose and, crucially, every one a new delight for the palate. Someone has tasted it and declared it worthy. It is rated 3rd best in the world and half the cost of Noma. They have a most reasonable wine list and treat you like a friend, not a cash cow. And it is a bloody sight warmer in Barcelona, even in February.
I still don't have a coat.

Disfrutar

For a long time Disfrutar has been my all time favourite venue, and, to me, defined what all top end dining should aspire to. I have made an annual pilgrimage to worship at the pass since it first opened its doors in 2014. The day after my first visit it was voted the best new restaurant in Europe. It is now rated the 3rd best in the world. It is the flagship restaurant of Mateu Casañas, Oriol Castro and Eduard Xatruch, originally heads of development at El Bulli, Ferran Adrià's legendary place in Roses on the Costa Brava. Alongside Adrià they gave birth to the molecular gastronomy movement or at least were the midwives.

Every Michelin stared restaurant now features spherification, usually in the form of a seemingly huge olive that bursts in your mouth with a flood of peppery olive oil or tiny little 'caviare' flavoured with some exotic fruit or whatnot. This all began in El Bulli. These chaps were in from the off and this is what you get in Disfrutar: Culinary magic tricks, grand gestures and amusing theatrics but never at the cost of undermining the taste. It is fine dining after all.

A bowl of black beans is shaken and out float little beetroot flying saucers. The fresh red and green peppers are actually of chocolate. Sweetcorn kernels have been painstakingly reconstructed, each one liquefied inside. You are invited to delve into a box of dry ice to see what you can discover hidden beneath the swirling mist. A white bread sandwich is really meringue. I could tell you more but I fear it may diminish your experience.

This is high table dining as performance art and you are part of the play, not stuck in the gods in your stuffed shirt. No tragedy here but a lot of drama fused with a light comedy, the waiters showmen, guiding your way through the script that has come from the kitchens. You wonder if one of them will be sawn in half as a finale.

Yet this is still a restaurant way ahead of the field. Upon arrival you are led through to the open plan kitchen where you are introduced to whichever head chefs and his team have time to pause with a good-hearted greeting. The service is warm, well informed and courteous. The front of house are true professionals and many have been there since the off. You are led to your table where your waiter introduces themselves by name. You are told to make yourselves at home and you feel that they genuinely mean it.

A friend, Jonas, recently visited twice within a fortnight The first time he was with his glamorous business partner, but all very innocent. A couple of weeks later he took his beautiful girlfriend. He was slightly put out that he was not acknowledged by the staff having previously got on quite friendly terms. However as soon as the lady took a bathroom break, the maître d' shot over and greeted him whole-heartedly. He had obviously been concerned about putting his foot in it in case of indiscretion on my friend's part who found it hysterical but admirable. That is the sign of a true professional.

There are only two choices on the menu, the Classic or the more experimental Festival, either of about 32 courses. However they are very flexible and go out of their way to accommodate any preferences, dietary, allergenic or otherwise. The plates are spectacular with extravagant and often theatrical presentation yet without pretension and, importantly, taste simply wonderful. You are given no indication of what will follow. A menu of what each item was, along with the wines, will only be given to you at the end. This is how it should be, sensation seekers. Just believe that each course will astound, thrill and delight. Just get on board, strap yourselves in and let go. It will be an escapade of a lifetime.

A wine pairing of sorts is offered but I tried this once and found this just too over the top. Rather than a glass of something matched to each course there were seemingly random, although I was told carefully chosen, offerings of strange liquids, many of which not wine at all. Saki, Cider, liqueurs, sherry. Fair enough but I do need some good conventional wine to wash my food down. In the end we had to order a couple of bottles of reliable Provence Rose to keep us going. I quite understand that this is in keeping with the quirky nature of the place but sometimes you just need refreshment.

The main room is a joy to be in, full of light, reminiscent of the seaside where the chefs come from, looking out on to a large enclosed terrace where coffee and digestifs are served. Sadly during my last visit I noticed that they had exchanged the beautiful tiled table tops for plain white linen cloths. I cheekily suggested, strongly denied, that this was perhaps a bid for the their third Michelin star that they clearly aspire to. I am sorry that it has so far eluded them, they clearly deserve it, but curiously I think it is better without it.

I have been to the only two 3* places in Barcelona and they are soulless, sterile affairs. At Lasarte, when I dropped my napkin, a waiter picked it up with chopsticks then presented a choice of 7 identical replacements proffered on a silver tray. If this is what it takes I don't need it.

At ABaC a junior sommelier outright refused to leave the bottle of wine on the table as I asked him to do so I could pour it myself. He said his boss would not allow it. I asked him just who he thought the was customer here and who was paying. Unperturbed he promised I would never have a dry glass. On the third time of waiting for a top up I just recovered it myself from where it had sat tantalisingly close and in full view. When he attempted to take it back I had to stab him with a fork. The second bottle was left where it should have been, at my fingertips. Don't fight with the clients; they have an array of sharp implements to hand.

During lockdown, once established it wasn't going away for a while, they produced a takeaway box of signature dishes. When restrictions were finally lifted Rubén Pol, Disfrutar's original Head Sommelier, brought a few of these to my restaurant for a private tasting with a few friends, alongside some premixed cocktails of his devising. Our chums, restaurateurs in their own right, complimented this extravagance with some very fine bottles of wine. That's my idea of a ready meal.
Still, not quite the experience of the real venue.
I shall be back.

DISFRUTAR - Carrer Villarroel, 163, Barcelona 08036

A spot of lunch in Barcelona ...

SUCULENT - Rambla del Raval 45, 08001
Spectacular experimental cuisine but very tasty for it at a most reasonable price. Go for the set menu. If you're lucky it might include rabbit brain on lobster tartare or Hare cannelloni and foie gras with crispy chicken skin.

LA MAR SALADA - Passeig Joan de Borbó, 58-59, 08003 Barceloneta
Set on a pretty terrace overlooking the harbour Albert goes to the fish auctions there every dawn to get the freshest produce. I have been eating here since the first week that I arrived in Barcelona when it was voted Best Lunch Menu in the Time Out food awards. One of the greatest combinations ever to pass my lips was here: A quail egg inside an artichoke heart topped with bone marrow and caviare. Rejoice!

COMPARTIR
When chefs Mateu Casañas, Oriol Castro and Eduard Xatruch left El Bulli, before Disfrutar (see above) they opened Compartir in Cadaqués on the Costa Brava. Now they have brought its little sister to Barcelona. Not so flamboyant as the flagship it is still creative gastronomy at a very reasonable price. Compartir means 'to share' and here the emphasis is, indeed, on sharing plates. Start with a selection of the divine oysters from the Ebro Delta. Other highlights include muscles in béarnaise sauce, veal carpaccio with port, foie gras and Idiazabal cheese and, foremost, crab with avocado and trout roe.

LA PLATILLERIA - Carrer Del Roser 82, 08004
Small tapas bar high up in Poble Sec but well worth the walk, this is some of the most stunning but unpretentious food to be had in Barcelona. Charming front of house from Mariela with husband Fernando manning the stove. The menu on a chalkboard doesn't hint at the complexity of tastes on offer. Try the quail in a jar (Codorniz), the meat and squid balls (Albondigas) or maybe the octopus (Pulpo) that just melts in your mouth. My absolute favourite, it just doesn't get much better.

BAR VICTORIA - Carrer dels Àngels, 8, 08001 Barcelona
A.A. Gill said that the best restaurant is your local that you go to the most. This is it for me. The lovely chaps here serve hearty Catalan favourites. Three courses and a bottle of wine each for 11 euros all in, day and night, you can't knock it. If you go on Sunday you just might find the Catalan classic Conill i cargols, rabbit and snails. Say hi from me.

SET PORTES - Pg. d'Isabel II, 14, 08003 Barcelona
Grand old school restaurant, open since 19C. Has the atmosphere of a gentlemen's club with a piano playing in the lobby and ancient waiters in black tie. Naturally very good paella. Authentic, not the tourist muck, with that all important socarrat, the crunchy layer on the bottom which all respectable paella must have. Great for a long lunch as they are open without a break so your afternoon can extend right into the evening as I have done on occasion.

Tips

112

'Ask not what you can do for your country. Ask what's for lunch.'
Orson Welles

LLAMBER - Carrer de la Fusina 5, El Born 08003
Creative funky sharing plates of curious combinations. Highlights could include Pulpo gratinado con queso ahumado de Pría, Morcilla de Burgos con chipirones or Foie con maiz en texturas but leave room for their stunning puddings.

EL XAMPANYET - Carrer de Montcada, 22, 08003 Barcelona
Old cava bar near the Picasso museum, it can get packed but worth popping by for a glass or three. Just make sure it is real Cava and not the cheap muck. The first time I went in the owner tried to sell me his bar cheaply on condition I took his wife with it.

CAN VILARÓ - Comte Borrell, 61, 08015 Barcelona
Family run old school Catalan restaurant. It serves the best brains in Barcelona. Quite literally. Deep fried in a panko coating. Order house wine and you'll be charged 2.50 for "Pa i Vi", bread and wine You certainly wouldn't have to sell your kidney but you could eat some. Offally good.

SALAMANCA - Carrer de l' Almirall Cervera, 34 Barceloneta
This is well established for groups that want tapas and paella at a reasonable price on a huge terrace. For my birthday I took 60 chums. I agreed a fee of 30 euros pp with the manager, including Pica Pica, paella, desserts, coffee, liquors and, amazingly all the beer, wine and cava we could drink. "You do realise a lot of the guests are English? " I asked. "I know" he replied with raised eyebrows and a mournful look as he saw the week's profits sail away. They did us proud.

LA CIUDADELA - Paseo Lluis Companys 08010
Handy if you are going to Parc Ciudadela opposite, this is the restaurant of a family run hotel. Great lunch menu on a terrace facing the Park for a tenner or an evening menu for a score and rooms upstairs if you can't make it home.

SESAMO - Carrer de Sant Antoni Abat, 52, 08001
The best vegetarian restaurant in town by far and good fun none the less. Run by the lovely Alfredo. Exceptional and imaginative fare all considered. Check the board behind the bar for exotic specials.

QUIMET Y QUIMET - Poeta Cabanyes 25, Poble Sec 08004
Tiny famous tapas bar tucked away in the back streets of Poble Sec. Very proud of their tinned food. The tins are presented on the plate to prove authenticity. Bless. Walls are covered in bottles you can drink there or take away.

RÍAS DO MIÑO - C/ de Pepe Rubianes, 37, 39, 08003 Barceloneta
Excellent value set lunch on a terrace by the beach. Galician seafood. Best fish soup in Barcelona. Authentic surly waiters. While having coffee one morning two paddy wagons pulled up and 20 Mossos, the local fuzz, rushed in. I assumed it was a raid but an hour later I found them packed into the basement laden with bottles of cava and brandy alongside plates of tapas. Just the night shift coming off duty.
"We're the Mossos and we haven't had our breakfast."

CIUDAD COMTAL - Rambla de Catalunya 18, 08007 Barcelona
Mouthwatering traditional tapas bar. Nice terrace on a rambla. Friendly staff. Elegant interior. You may have to queue, it's the national hobby, but worth the wait. Grab the man in the blue shirt and put your name down. Open until 1.30am every day of the year.

CERVECERIA CATALANA - Carrer Mallorca, 236, Barcelona
Sister to Ciudad Comtal above but a bit further uptown. Same deal, Same grub. Top gaf.

TAPAC24 - Carrer de la Diputació, 269 Barcelona
Offshoot of the now closed Comerc24 from the charming and creative chef Carles Abellan. It's tapas with a twist. Try McFoie Burger or truffle oil Bikini. Other branches around town.

DOBLE ZER00 - Carrer de Jaume Giralt, 53 08003 Barcelona
Funky tapas and sushi Japanese restaurant. Great value sashimi set lunch and some quite odd jap/spanish fusion on la carte. Foie wonton with caramelised mango and Eel, anyone?

BARLOVENTO - Rambla Poblenou, 21, 08005
Seemingly upmarket but good value restaurant out of the centre in Poble Nou. Lift up to a large terrace upstairs, covered and heated in winter. Interesting tapas and seminal Catalan specials such as Trotters with Crab claws and Snails. Great rib steaks. It's the real thing.

ELSA & FRED - Rec Comtal 11, 08003
French bistro decor, funky food. Oxtail burger a must.

VIVANDA - Major de Sarrià, 134, Sarrià-Sant Gervasi, Barcelona 08017
Tucked away far up town in Sarrià, this hidden gem, sister restaurant to Alkimai, features a cool and lush garden. Food, served in small portions ideal for sharing, is creative and seasonal and may feature superb snails and a very spicy steak tartar. A magical place all round. Definitely worth a detour.

SHUNKA - Sagristans, 5, 08002
Best Japanese in town. Behind the Cathedral. Favourite of Ferran Adrià and other top chefs.
Now has a sister restaurant Koy Shunka serving fusion.

GELIDA - Diputació, 133, 08015 (corner of Urgell) Google Map
You don't get a more authentic old school Catalan eating experience than this, or cheaper. Cap i Pota, Galtes de Porc, Miel i Mato & trifásico did it for me. Probably the best snails in town too. The vino comes in a porró straight from the barrel and you have to ask for a glass if you don't want to neck it from the spout as you should do. It felt like asking for a knife and fork in a Chinese restaurant but I've made a mess of a good shirt before.
There is no menu del dia but the most expensive dish to be had is 4.50€. Wine 2.30€ a carafe and the bill is down to your honesty. You just tell them what you had as they tot it up at the end.

A good sardine is always better than a mediocre lobster.
Ferran Adrià

114

... AND DINNER IN LONDON

London is awash with fine opportunities to lunch, my preferred eating hour, though sadly some favourite old haunts didn't make it through the plague. These old survivors hung on in there. Let's lunch.

ST JOHNS - 26 St John St, ECIM 4AY,
Fergus and Trevor's original temple to Great British Food; the place that redefined the UK dining scene for years to come and still one of the finest. Pure simple dishes utilising well sourced produce. Personalty I prefer eating in the bar rather than the noisy main room. Roast Bone Marrow with Parsley Salad is essential or share a whole Pig's Head with your chums, ripping it apart with your paws.

ROCHELLE CANTEEN - 16 Playground Gardens, London E2 7FA,
Set in the playground in what may have been the old bicycle shed of an old school, you have to ring a discrete doorbell by the Boys entrance, this is Margot Henderson (AKA Mrs Fergus) & Melanie Arnold's love-child. Go in the summer when the tables are dragged outside into the sunshine. The menu, as you might expect, is British and fresh seasonal flavours abound. A peaceful hidden sanctuary away from the London rush.

Sadly they now have a drinks licence as before it was BYOB. On one memorable occasion Farika produced a bottle of Gordon's, tonic water, lemon slices, a set of glasses, a bag of ice and bitters, all from her Mary Poppins style carpetbag to the astonishment of the guests and staff alike.

THE CLOVE CLUB - 380 Old St, London ECI
Rated the UK's highest in The World's Best Restaurants, and deservedly so, this is British fare with a twist using the best quality produce and some scarce ingredients, Very classy yet it still retains a relaxed unstuffy atmosphere. Just make sure you're not paying.

One year on my birthday they offered BYOB without corkage. We had a private room and a dedicated sommelier who even called the week before to see if anything needed decanting. Now that is good service.

ESCOFFIER ROOM - Vincent Rooms, 76 Vincent Square, London SWIP 2PD
Westminster Kingsway Catering College's restaurant tucked away in the smarter end of Victoria, this is where the students learn and practice their art. In the more formal Escoffier Room you are offered a seasonally themed set menu, changing weekly. Only open in term times. Seven course tasting menu for 40 quid. Good wine list with low markups.

BRAT - 4 Redchurch St, London E1 6JL,
Up a discrete staircase this used to be the back room of what was the strip club below. Ignore all the wood fired meats and whole turbot unless you have brought your bank manager. Just order lots of smaller plates to share, Spider Crab Toast, Sweetbreads, Moorland Beef Tartare - all of them probably. Claims it is Spanish influenced but seems very British to me. Great food either way. Recently awarded a well deserved Michelin star.
Second more informal branch in Hackney with huge covered courtyard. (374 Helmsley Place, E8 3SB)

RANOUSH JUICE - 43 Edgware Road, London W2 2JE
I love lamb breast, spread whole with fruit stuffing, rolled up and slow baked, but it is now almost impossible to get hold of. The answer is kebabs, not those hideous grey elephant feet you see with a closing time queue at midnight but the authentic Levantine bars, in this case Lebanese.
This is the kebab you eat when you are NOT drunk. A real treat and worth crossing town or at least walking the length of Oxford Street, to find out what can be done. Mostly takeaway they do have a few tables outside but in the summer grab one and amble down to Hyde Park nearby. Importantly not forgetting a Ranoush Juice itself, seemingly made from carrots it tastes curiously of strawberries. You go figure.

THE FRENCH HOUSE - 49 Dean St, W1
The French, for me, is home from home. I lived in the same block, almost above it, for a few years. The restaurant upstairs has been the starting point for some of London's finest. Fergus and Margo Henderson cut their teeth here alongside Jon Spiteri, London's most charming and influential maître d'. Now Neil Borthwick, husband to Angela Hartnett, is behind the pass or, in this case, backstairs.
Classic French countryside fare made British.

TSIAKKOS & CHARCOAL - 5 Marylands Rd, W9 2DU
No really. It is open. it just looks like it shut up shop and hasn't been occupied for 30 years. Faded curtains in the window, it gives the impression that if you did go in you may come across something you shouldn't and leave in a body bag. Let's just say that it is part of its charm. Once inside, although fairly makeshift, it is rather cosy even though the roof has clearly been jerry-rigged as and when it was needed and might not hold back a decent storm. However a warm atmosphere extends across the room from an intimate crowd.

THE INDIA CLUB - 143 Strand, WC2R 1JA,
There are many far better places if you're after a decent curry but nowhere with such a transformative atmosphere.
Opening over 50 years ago it doesn't appear to have been redecorated since. Yet it does not just tolerate its shabbiness but boasts of it on the website. If not for lunch go late afternoon for their curious cocktails.

Dominating this is the owner who greets you as a long lost friend and treats you like his brother. This is my kind of gaff. It is for a lot of post shift chefs too apparently. This is how your local restaurant should be and you are planning to return before you've sat down to eat. The fare is substantial Greek home cooking that would shame no Hellenic grandmother. It is just perfect. Now you are returning tomorrow. Just don't tell anyone. NB Cash only, of course. It had to be.

A WONG - 70 Wilton Rd, SW1V 1DE
After studying chemistry at Oxford then social anthropology at the LSE, Andrew Wong returned to his parents' Cantonese and transformed it into what is now one of only two two-starred Michelin Chinese restaurants outside Asia. Far away from your average high-street Chinese, go with a large group so you can experience more dishes, for the lunchtime Dim Sum which may include Foie Gras or Wagyu Beef, each little morsel taking you to a higher plane.

YMCA INDIAN STUDENT HOSTEL - 41 Fitzroy Square, London, W1T 6AQ,
By far the cheapest curry in the west end and no less for it, it doesn't get more authentic than this.

THE QUALITY CHOP HOUSE - 88-94 Farringdon Rd. London, ECIR 3EA
Opened in 1869 I used to go here for a breakfast fry-up most days when I had a studio in Clerkenwell in the 80s. It was a proper greasy spoon then, the Mexican chef bent over the flat top, ash dropping from his huge cigar onto the grill, When it sadly shut up it was turned into a nose-to-tail diner by restaurateur Will Lander and extended next door, the beautiful wood panelled booths seamlessly reproduced to match the originals. A bit out of my price range now but their Sunday Roast Lunch is legendary.

THE EAGLE - 159 Farringdon Rd London, ECIR 3AL
Bang opposite the Quality Chop House this is the place that began the gastropub revolution in 1991. The grill at the end of the bar cooks up classic dishes as well as they did when David Eyre first opened it. I don't know if he knew what he had started but it still stands out from millions of imitators. I recall seeing a pre-fame Graham Norton doing a cabaret upstairs dressed as a nun in a habit and wimple made from bar cloths. Gets packed every weekend,

CLIPSTONE - 5 Clipstone Street, London W1
Tucked away behind BBC Broadcasting House among the rag trade, off Great Portland Street, this is a sister restaurant to the Quality Chop House though you'd never guess. Modern Scandinavian design with bum aching seats. I used to go just for the brains. Small sharing plates of modern European/British menu. Reasonable value for such quality fare. Dreamy whipped cod's roe, rich venison tartar and Paris-Brest, a heart attack waiting to happen.

HUNAN - 51 Pimlico Road, London SW1W 8NE
A complete Chinese/Taiwanese blow-out but of the highest quality. No menu, they just ask you what you don't like then Chef Peng, tucked away in the basement, starts knocking quite unique dishes out as he sees fit until you're stuffed.
Then they ask if you want lobster.

Very reasonable wine list. £60 for lunch, £90 in the evening. Don't eat breakfast beforehand. A real treat.

10 GREEK STREET - 10 Greek Street, London W1D 4DH
Great little place in Soho. Seasonal modern British food with European touches from a daily changing menu. Pigs cheeks, Monkfish cheeks, Octopus and the like. Great wine list with low mark-ups. Ask for the 'little black book', a hand-written list of rarer wine gems if you want to push the boat out. You can't book in the evening but turn up early, give them your phone number while you go to the pub and they'll give you a bell when your table is ready.

ROTI KING - 40 Doric Way, London NW1 1LH
Outstanding Malaysian food. They have branched out now to other venues but the original in a basement in Euston is the one for its tatty charm. There is still the sign for the laundry it was before outside. Watching the chef cooking and stretching the roti is theatre in itself. Fantastic Beef Rendang but wear a bib, at least I need to. No booking, you have to queue. BYOB from M&S in Euston station opposite.

It is more fun to talk with someone who doesn't use long, difficult words
but rather short, easy words like: 'What about lunch?'
Winnie-the-Pooh

Just Don't

In the Bar

Don't wave money at the bartender. We are all going to have to get our wallets out in the end but you won't need yours for a while now you are back of the queue, twat. The only thing worse is snapping your fingers. Now you are back of the queue forever. There was a great barmaid at Le Quecumbar, who, when a punter snapped his fingers at her from the other end of the bar, snarled, "Sorry, love, it takes more than two fingers to make me come".

Don't hit on the waitresses. She is being friendly because she's good at her job even if you are a twat.

Don't order cocktails in a pub. They won't be good and you'll look a twat.

Don't ask your friends what they want just when you're asked for your order, twat.

Don't ask to change the music. If you want to listen to your own playlist go home and play it there.

Don't, ever, fucking ever, try to get behind the jump. This applies even more so to the kitchen pass. Chefs have very sharp instruments and very hot liquids to remind you.

Don't try to sneak in with a group if you have been barred. If you have genuine remorse go in on a quiet afternoon, have a word and apologise. They may reconsider. If so say thank you and buy the barman a drink. But then you probably got barred for being a twat so this is unlikely

In Restaurants

Don't try to split the bill individually. It is rude, wastes time and it will always be short.
Work it out with your table, however you wish, then present the full amount.

Don't bitch about your meal on social media when you left smiling. If you have a genuine complaint we will take it very seriously and, if fact, appreciate it. Don't even wait until the end. If there is something wrong with your food, tell the waiter. We will change it. If there is something wrong with the waiter, tell the manager. We want you to leave happy and can't do that if you just gripe the day after.

Don't give a one star review on Google just because we were shut on the day you came, despite listing that we always do. I have genuinely seen this more that once along the lines "I came on a Monday. There was a sign on the door saying 'Closed on Mondays'. I checked on the website and it said so too. Likewise Google" One star!!

Don't wait until the food arrives to announce your allergies.

Don't join a group just when they are just finishing the meal and expect dinner when the kitchen is already shut.

Don't fail to cancel your reservation, however late.
Remember, we have your phone number. If it happens more that once I will write it on the wall of a public toilet.

I spotted a very striking water feature near the entrance to Hakkasan
in the form of a man relieving himself over some bin bags while chatting on the phone
Tracey MacLeod

FOR RESTAURANTS

Don't shut the coffee machine off before the end of service or at least until you have shut the bar. Believe me, I would love to and possibly may have done so but it is the last thing anyone orders and, anyway, it is a huge mark-up.

Don't charge insane mark-ups on wine. This particularly applies in the UK where four or five hundred percent is not uncommon. I know everyone else does it but isn't doubling the retail price enough when all you are doing is opening a bottle and washing the glasses? Nowadays everyone has Vivino app and can immediately see what you are up to.

Don't leave me thirsty. As soon as the customer is seated at the table, ask them if they would like to order drinks even if they are the first of the party. Maybe they don't want anything but get that order if you can. I cannot even read a menu without a glass of wine.

Don't attempt to remember the order. It will inevitably be wrong. It always is. What is wrong with pen and paper or digital input straight to the EPOS?

Don't start taking plates away until the last person is finished. This is a tricky one as we all know someone who could still be on the starter, jabbering away, when we are on the coffee but just ask.

Don't sit down at my table or, for that matter, slap me on the back unless we are familiar. I want us to have a happy relationship but we need to keep a certain degree of respect.

Don't only stock big brand draft lager just because you are given umbrellas for your terrace. You know it's shit. Sure they give you a good price if you agree not to stock others but there is a reason it's cheap. That is why all the other pubs have it. I appreciate that half your punters are ignoramuses but many others will notice and return.

Don't just stock Schweppes tonic. It's crap. Get some decent tonic in. Charge a premium if you have to.

Don't make people wait a long time for the bill. They now want to leave and you may just turn over the table again if you're lucky. It may affect your tip too.

Don't forget to offer your customers a shot of something as they leave. This is quite common in Spain and Italy but the UK have failed to adopt it. It could well be something cheap and nasty. Limoncello or the lighter fuel known as Oruko will do. Perhaps have a bottle of a strange concoction that you keep in the freezer for that purpose; try a few stems of Bison Grass in a supermarket vodka. Don't give them a choice though or they'll expect better. The offer, however, will be appreciated if nothing else, and cost you little. Importantly, if you do so, make sure you offer it to all and sundry, not just a few elites, or resentment will ensue.

"We want our table back in 90 minutes". Do you now?
"Well excuse me but I came for lunch and I am here for the duration. I thought it was a restaurant." **119**

Playlist – Intimate Dinner for Two

Vladimir Cosma | Promenade sentimentale
Erik Satie: London Symphony Orchestra | Gymnopedie No. 1
Erik Satie: Klara Kormendi | 3 Gymnopédies: Gymnopedie No. 1
Wilhelmenia Fernandez: London Philharmonic Orchestra | La Wally
Vladimir Cosma | Promenade sentimentale
Beaver & Krause | Walkin'
Beaver & Krause | Good Places
Éric Serra | Lucia di lammermoor
Erik Satie: Klara Kormendi | Gnossienne No.1: Lent
Johann Sebastian Bach: Yo-Yo Ma | Cello Suite No. 1 in G Major,Léo
Delibes: Opera-Comique | Delibes: Lakmé
Ludwig van Beethoven: Symphony No. 9 in D minor
Wolfgang Amadeus Mozart | The Marriage of Figaro
Beaver & Krause | By Your Grace
Beaver & Krause | Short Film for David
Philip Glass: Michael Riesman | Facades
Philip Glass: Philip Glass Ensemble | Glassworks: I. Opening
Maurice Ravel: Isao Tomita | Boléro
Lang Lang | Gnossiennes: Gnossiennes No. 1 - Lent
Éric Serra: Inva Mula | Lucia di lammermoor
Gabriel Yared | 37°2 le matin
Beaver & Krause | Another Part of Time
Johann Sebastian Bach | Bach, JS: Cello Suite No. 1 in G Major
Penguin Cafe Orchestra | Perpetuum Mobile
Lalo Schifrin | Jim On The Move
John Barry | On Her Majesty's Secret Service - Remastered
John Barry Orchestra | Space March (Capsule In Space)
John Barry Orchestra | The Girl with the Sun in Her Hair
John Barry | Thunderball
John Barry | The Ipcress File
John Barry | Midnight Cowboy
John Barry | Big Fella
Esquivel, His Piano and Group | Begin the Beguine
Esquivel! | Sentimental Journey
Esquivel! | Latin-Esque
Esquivel! | Mucha Muchacha
Esquivel! | Surfboard
Lund Quartet | Lonn
Martin Denny | Llama Serenade

https://tdy.es/eqjUg

Playlist - Micheladas & Tacos for Ten

Lou Reed - New Sensations
Mano Negra - Out of Time Man
Madness - One Step Beyond - 2009 - Remaster
The Specials - Ghost Town - 2015 Remaster
Norma Tanega - You're Dead
ESG - Dance
Roxy Music - Do The Strand
Grandmaster Flash: Grandmaster Melle Mel - White Lines (Don't Do It)
Funkadelic - Can You Get to That
J.J. Cale - Travelin' Light
Tricky - Hell Is Round The Corner
Madeleine Peyroux - Tango Till They're Sore
Tommy McCook: The Supersonics - Ska Jam
Jazz Jamaica - Monkey Man
Ska Cubano - Soy Campesino
Stereo MC's - Connected
Parquet Courts - Freebird II
Alan Vega - Juke Box Baby
Ian Dury - Wake Up And Make Love With Me
Buddy Rich Big Band - The Beat Goes On - Live At Chez Club,
Hollywood/1966/Remix
Prince Buster - One Step Beyond
Toots & The Maytals - Broadway Jungle
Linton Kwesi Johnson - Inglan Is A Bitch
Nina Simone - Funkier Than a Mosquito's Tweeter
Ian Dury - Clevor Trever
Shirley Bassey - Jezahel - 2000 Remaster
Jonathan Richman - I Was Dancing In The Lesbian Bar
Martha and the Muffins - Echo Beach
Ocean Colour Scene - Hundred Mile High City
Fun Lovin' Criminals - Couldn't Get It Right
The Frightnrs - Sharon
Sharon Jones & The Dap-Kings - Inspiration Information
Link Wray - Jack the Ripper
MC5 - The American Ruse
Small Faces - You Need Loving
Paul Williams - You Give A Little Love
Traffic - The Low Spark Of High-Heeled Boys
Doc Watson - Deep River Blues

https://tdy.es/IHdUa

I have always suspected that my ice cream is, in fact,
made out of frozen glops of pig fat, soya beans and fish oil.
Peter Cook

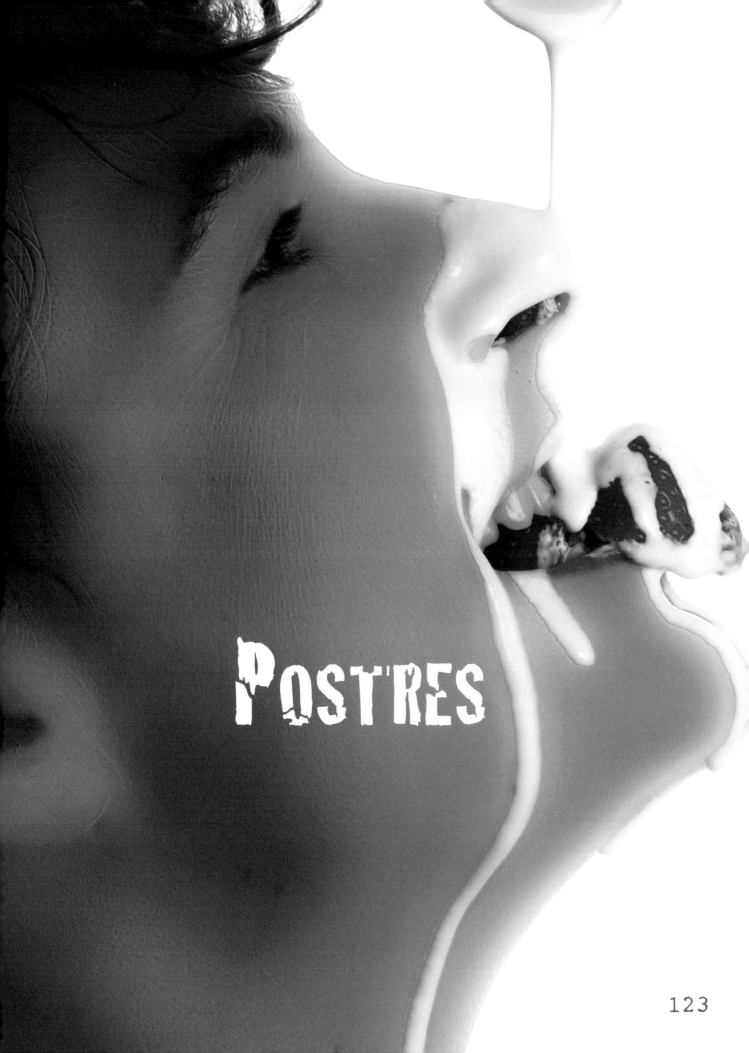

POSTRES

Beetroot Sorbet

Works well as an accompaniment to both a plate of cold meats or a dish of sweetened red fruits, or just as a palate cleanser between courses.

- Packet of pre-steamed beetroot (500 g)
- ½ tsp Rose water
- 3 tbsp Agave syrup,
- 20 ml Lemon juice
- 1 tsp Tara gum

Blend everything and sieve through fine muslin.
Chill then churn in an ice cream maker.
Freeze for at least a couple of hours before serving.

Foie Gras Ice cream

I know, I know. Foie Gras, yeah!
If it is not for you I quite understand. Just move on.
But this is the most luscious ice cream ever made.
Try a little sharp blue cheese on the side to cut through the richness and a bottle of Chateau d'Yquem if you're feeling very extravagant.

Cover your head with a napkin to hide yourself from the eyes of god and enjoy.

- 300 g Raw foie gras
- 60 ml Pedro Ximénez sherry
- 60 g Sugar
- 4 egg yolks
- 250 ml Heavy cream
- 1 level tsp Tara gum, if available

Devein the Foie Gras and vacuum seal.
Sous Vide for 2 hours at 56°C.

Whisk the egg yolks and sugar then slowly drizzle in the cream, whisking as you go. In a pan at low heat very gradually bring the mixture to 85°C but no more, constantly stirring to make a crème anglaise. In a separate pan reduce the sherry to half original volume. Allow both to cool.

In a liquidiser, on low power, blend the Foie Gras, sherry and custard, sprinkling in the Tara gum as you go,

Chill in the fridge then churn in an ice cream maker.
Freeze for at least 4 hours.

To serve, dust with pure cacao powder and crumble a bit of sharp blue cheese around the edge of the plate. Accompany with a glass of PX or good Sauternes.

Toast and Marmalade Ice Cream

This has been a real winner.
It came about from getting the Toast flavouring provided by maestro mixologist Sam Sareen.
It is only available from cocktail suppliers so you will have to hunt around.

- 6 Egg yolks
- 100 g Sugar
- 500 ml Cream
- 200 m Crème fraîche
- 1 level tsp Tara gum
- 340 g Tip Tree orange marmalade
- Toast concentrate

Heat both creams in a pan. Whisk egg and sugar; Gradually add hot cream to egg mix. Slowly whisk in Tara gum

Heat all this in pan to 86°C, constantly stirring, to form custard. Shock with iced water under pan to cool. Add marmalade and a good squirt of Toast concentrate. Stir well. Process in ice cream maker for about 50 minutes.

Decant to a Tupperware container and leave in the freezer for at least 4 hours.

Stout Ice Cream

- 500 ml Sweet stout
- 300 g Sugar
- 250 g Butter
- 750 ml Cream
- 6 Egg yolks
- 1 tsp Malvern salt
- 1 tsp Tara gum

Heat the sugar with two tablespoons of water, on high. Allow it to caramelise undisturbed until it is a rich, dark amber. Let it smoke for a few seconds, then quickly stir in the butter on low. Gently stir in the cream.
Slowly sift the Tara gum in, constantly stirring.

Whisk the egg yolks until very well combined.
Add the dairy mixture to yolks, one ladle at a time, whisking constantly, then the yolk mixture likewise. Cook on low heat, stirring frequently, until the custard thickens to coat the back of a spoon and a swiped finger leaves a clean line.

Very slowly heat the stout in a pan and reduce by half. Remove from heat and stir the beer into the custard.

Add a generous amount of rock salt to taste.
Cool then churn in an ice cream maker and freeze.

127

Pa, Xocolata, oli d'oliva i sal

Pa, Xocolata, oli d'oliva i sal , a traditional Catalan dessert, of toast, chocolate, olive oil and salt, dates from the civil war when luxury fare was scarce and had to be spun out.

It is a sort of savoury version of Pa amb Tomàquet and, in the same way, you are often just given the ingredients and expected to fend for yourself.

This is a slightly grander version.

- 250 g 85% chocolate
- 250 g Fresh cream
- 50 g Toasted pistachio nuts
- 100 ml Very spicy olive oil

Dry blend the chocolate in a liquidiser to chop it up. Separately blend the nuts to chop them coarsely then combine.

Slowly heat cream to near boiling then pour over chocolate and nuts mix.
Stir it together as the chocolate melts
Sprinkle a cautious pinch of hot pepper and a decent pinch of salt flakes
Set in fridge for a few hours

Plate using a small ice cream scoop.
Pour spicy olive oil around the edge, not over it
Generously sprinkle with salt flakes and a touch more pepper to taste.
Serve hot bread or Melba toast on the side.

Mint and Black Pepper Pineapple

1 Fresh pineapple, peeled
1 tsp Madagascan peppercorns, crushed
1/3 cup Brown Sugar
A handful mint leaves
A pinch of salt

Chop up pineapple into chunks.
Vacuum seal with sugar and mint.
Sous Vide at 66°C for 12 hours.
Shock with ice and refrigerate.

Serve with a pinch of wild pepper,
a drop of Crème fraîche
and a couple of fresh mint leaves

HORCHATA & BLACK RICE PUDDING

Horchata de Chufa is a popular Spanish drink made from Tiger Nuts.
If you can't find it then Coconut milk works well.

- 250 g Thai Black Rice
- 125 g Sugar
- 400 ml Horchata, low sugar if possible
- or reduce the amount of sugar

Soak rice for 40 minutes then drain and rinse.
Bring rice, 3 cups water, and ¼ teaspoon salt to a boil then simmer on low heat for 45 minutes.
Stir in sugar, good pinch of salt, and the Horchata.

Simmer, uncovered, stirring occasionally, until mixture is thick, about 30 minutes.
Chill until cold then store in a fridge overnight.
Serve with a drizzle of Horchata and coconut flakes.

Fennel Ice

This works equally well accompanying a salad, fish or as a palate cleanser.

Reserve the fronds for decoration once made.

Take:
- 500 ml Cream
- 200 ml Crème fraîche
- 250 g Chopped fennel
- 2 tsp Fennel seeds, crushed
- Lemon zest

Simmer above in pan for 30 mins then let cool and sieve.

Beat together:
4 egg yolks
150 g Caster Sugar

Slowly mix eggs with cream mix. (You don't want scrambled eggs.) Simmer until you get a custard constituency. Sieve a level tsp Tara gum powder over the mix and stir well.

Leave to cool then churn in an ice cream maker. Set in a freezer.

DRINK!

If I had all the money I spent on drink, I'd spend it on drink.

Vivian Stanshall - Sir Henry at Rawlinson End

All cocktails herein are the work of maestro George Mulholland.

So is the artwork opposite

@george.h.mulholland

GROS

COCKTAILS

10 EUROS

NEGRONI
Ginebra, Vermut, Aperol

DARK & STORMY
Havana Club 7, Cerveza de Jengibre, Angostu...

MANHATTAN
...Vermut, Angostu...

...CUBANO
...mout, Dis. Ronno, Coffee S...

...PRESS... MARTINI
Vodka, Kah...

PACHARAN...
Pacharan, Limón, Hierba...

THE STOUT CUBANO

- 50 ml Havana 7 Rum
- 50 ml La Calavera Original Medical Stout
- 25 ml Gomme
- 50 ml Egg white

Shake everything with ice.
Strain into large wine glass with a fresh cube of ice.

Pisco Sour

- 75 ml Pisco
- 25 ml Fresh lime juice
- 25 ml Gomme
- 50 ml Egg white
- Angostura bitters

Shake vigorously and strain.
Serve with a twist of lime and top with a dash of Angostura.

Sangria Blanca

- 25 ml Mascaró V.O. Brandy
- 25 ml St~Germain Elderflower liqueur
- Freshly squeezed orange juice
- Cava

Stir brandy, St~Germain and orange juice in a pint glass.
with plenty of ice cubes and a slice of orange.
Top up with a good Cava.

Patxaran Sour

- 50 ml Patxaran Gaizka
- 25 ml Cointreau
- 25 ml Lemon juice
- 25 ml Gomme
- 50 ml Egg white
- Dash Orange bitters

Shake vigorously
Serve with an orange twist

Louis Armstrong once said "There is two kinds of music, the good, and the bad. I play the good kind. "

For us the same goes for food and drink. Learning to see the possible good in something you dislike is an important lesson.

Take patxaran for example. Made with sloe berries from the blackthorn bush in El País Basco and Navarra, one doesn't immediately jump at the idea of knocking back a glass of the intense fruit and herb tasting beverage.

That said it was a challenge and we do like a challenge. After creating a fabulous cocktail with the most common brand of patxaran, Zoco, personally undrinkable to me on its own, we naturally pushed on.

There is a moment in a bartender's career when one can only do so much, and it seems only a higher quality liquor will quench that thirst for unachievable perfection. The Patxaran we eventually used for this cocktail, Patxaran Gaizka, is family made and sold directly, even coming with a personally signed thank you note.

And, not to forget, very drinkable.

*George

136

Bourbon Amaretto Sour

- 60 ml Bulleit Bourbon
- 20 ml Disaronno Amaretto
- 25 ml Fresh lime juice
- 20 ml Gomme
- 50 ml Egg white

Shake vigorously.
Serve with a slice of orange
and a dash of orange bitters

Pink Buffalo

- 75 ml Zubrówka Bison Grass Vodka
- 20 ml Fresh lime juice
- 1 bottle Fever-Tree Mediterranean tonic water
- 2 Dried hibiscus flowers
- 2 Dried raspberries

Stir vodka, lime, hibiscus and raspberries in a glass with ice.
Top up with tonic.

138

Dark and Stormy 1919

- 75 ml Angostura 1919 Rum
- Bottle of Fever Tree Ginger Beer
- Large dash of Angostura bitters
- Wedge of lime

When it comes to classics, more often than not they are simple yet effective. How does one then improve or leave your mark? How do you make it great? This comes down to great produce, not necessarily expensive, but more a thirst for knowledge. Information is key and you are your best source.

*George

Nathan Barley

- 50 ml Angostura 1919 Rum
- 50 ml Egg white
- 25 ml Gomme
- Rondadora and La Montnegre English Barley Wine

Shake rum, egg and gomme with ice.
Pour into large brandy glass with one cube of ice.
Top up with Barley Wine.

THE INDEPENDENT

- 50 ml Ratafia dels Raiers
- 10 ml Kahlúa
- 20 ml Grey Goose Vodka
- 50 ml Full fat milk
- Tonka Beans (or nutmeg if not available)

Add the Ratafia and Kahlúa to a Margarita Glass.
Shake the vodka and milk with a cube of ice.
Finely strain, slowly pouring into the glass, floating on top. Grate a dusting of tonka bean on top with a microplane.

Allow the client to stir it themselves before drinking.

Following our success with the infamous Patxaran we wondered what dusty back shelf bottle we could spice up next.

After failing miserably with my arch enemy, the Italian "Fernet Branca", commonly known as the chefs' drink, along came Ratafia.

A local, old school Catalan digestive made from various fruits, walnuts and herbs, this drink was equally unappealing to me as Patxaran. Yet, there was hope. Deep down I knew I could use this. I knew I needed to dilute the intense flavour and it would work with coffee or milk or both. So naturally I thought ... White Russian.

From there, through the usual process of trial, error and rosy cheeks, we eventually came up with "The Independent".

A stand alone cocktail.
A Catalan cocktail.
Made by an Englishman.

*George

El Diablo

- 20 ml Gabriel Boudier Crème de Cassis de Dijon
- Bottle of Fever Tree Ginger Beer
- 50 ml El Jimador tequila
- ½ Freshly squeezed lime
- Dash of Orange Bitters

Serve with lime twist
and 2 dried raspberries

Pimms Mojito

- 85 ml Pimm's Cup No. 1
- 20 ml Lemon Juice
- 20 ml Gomme
- 10 ml Elderflower cordial diluted with 30 ml soda water
- Handful of fresh mint leaves

Muddle mint and gomme
Add Pimms and lemon then shake
Strain over ice and top up with cordial
Dress with a few mint leaves and a slice of lemon

142

Apple Brumble

- 4 Granny Smith Apples, peeled, cored and chopped
- 4 tbsp Brown sugar
- 1 stick Cinnamon
- 1 Vanilla pod
- 1500 ml Cider
- 400 ml Brandy
- 1½ Lemons
- 1 Orange
- Tonka bean (or nutmeg if not available)

In a pan, over a medium heat, stir sugar until it caramelises.
Add apples, cinnamon, vanilla and the juice of one lemon until the apples soften and brown.
Keep on a low simmer and slowly add the cider then the brandy.

Set aside a few apple slices then sieve the rest, squeezing all the liquid out.
Return the reserved apples to the liquid.
Keep hot in a crock-pot until ready to serve.
Finely grate tonka bean over the glass.

Negroni Sour

- 50 ml Gin
- 50 ml Vermut
- 50 ml Aperol
- 50 ml Egg white
- 25 ml Fresh lime juice
- 20 ml Gomme

Shake everything with one ice cube.
Strain over 2 ice cubes
Serve with an orange twist and a dash of Orange Bitters

ESPRESSO MARTINI

So here we have it.
Probably the most famous cocktail ever.
Created by the greatest bartender and a true gentleman, Mr Dick Bradsell.
A legend in his own drinking-up time.

He adamantly disliked the term mixologist or even barman.
He was, as far as he was concerned, a bartender; that is what he had done since the In and Out. Tend bars.
What a great job he did of it too.

A great phrase of his was "Don't make me not like you".
It may have been slung my way on occasion.
He did not suffer fools gladly. A necessary quality behind the jump.
Sadly missed but his legacy lives on throughout the libatious world and beyond

There are so many versions of his definitive and notorious cocktail.
This is just our take.
Please raise a glass in his memory.
*Oli

- 50 ml Grey Goose Vodka
- 25 ml Kahlúa
- Double shot of cold press high roast coffee

Allow coffee to cool if hot.
Shake everything with ice.
Strain into a chilled Martini glass.

For more of Dick, please read his unique book,
'Dicktales or Thankyous and Sluggings'

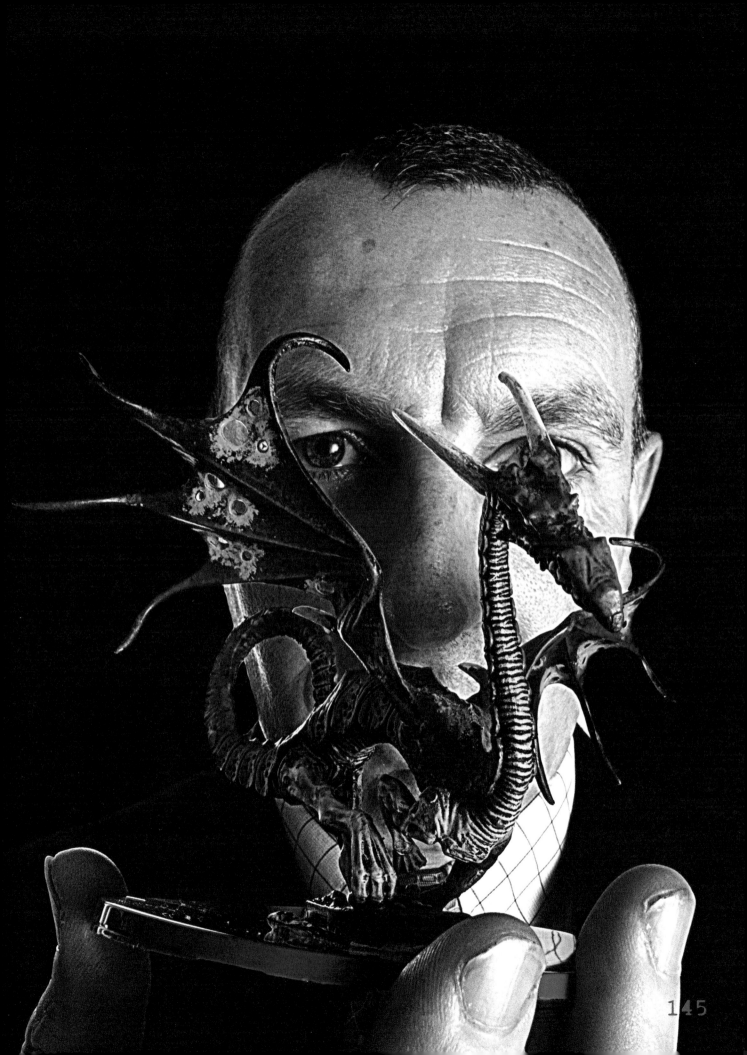

Two gentlemen comparing their plums

The Kitchen Cupboard

Good Olive Oil

Chicken Stock Cubes

Bisto Granules

Cartons of Tomato Frito/ Passata

Toasted Almonds

Lemon Juice or Citric Acid

Jar of Horseradish

Colman's Mustard Powder

Harissa paste

Bottle of Lee & Perrins

Powdered Milk

Arrowroot & Cornflower

Smash

Barry's Tea

Marmite

Heinz Ketchup

Kraft Mayonnaise

Maple Syrup (the real stuff)

Agave Syrup

Natural Liquid Stevia

Gentleman's Relish

Tube of Anchovy Paste

Can of Calabrian Anchovies

Cholula Hot Chipotle Salsa

Can of Chipotle Peppers

Trufflehunter White Truffle Oil

Beetroot powder

Dried Porcini Mushrooms

De Cecco Spaghetti no. 12

Chinese White Vinegar

Japanese Sushi Vinegar

Ketjap Manis (sweet soy)

Cooking Soy

Light Table Soy

Sesame Oil

Walnut oil

Pomegranate Molasses

Ginger & Garlic Paste

Tinned Coconut Milk

Patak's Hot Lime Pickle

Fennel Seeds

Cumin Powder

Dried Thyme

Dried Oregano

Herbes de Provence

Paprika

Chilli Flakes

Malvern Salt Flakes

Madagascan pepper

Tonka Beans

Tara Gum

Xanthan gum

Dried Puy Lentils

Dried Red Lentils

Dried Peas

Yellow Dahl

Jar of White Beans

Bulgur Wheat

THE COCKTAIL CABINET

Nordés Galician Gin

Tanqueray Sevilla Gin

Beefeater Gin

Bulleit Rye

Laphroaig Isley Single Malt

Cardenal Mendoza

Angostura 1919 Rum

Pujol Barcelona Rum

Captain Morgan Spiced Rum

Pussers Gunpowder Proof Rum 54.5%

Stolichnaya Vodka

Grey Goose Vodka

Zubrowka Bison Grass Vodka

Corralejo Reposado Tequila

Patrón XO Cafe Liqueur

Disaronno Amaretto

Barsol Pisco

Linie Aquavit

Patxaran Gaizka

Pimm's No.1

Vermut Espinaler 125 Aniversario

St. Germain Elderflower Liqueur

Heritier Cassis

Campari

Kahlua

Baileys

Cointreau

Aperol

Fever-Tree Mediterranean Tonic

Fever-Tree Ginger Beer

R. White's Lemonade

Coca Cola - 200ml glass bottles

Soda Syphon

Bottle of Egg White

Home Made Simple Syrup

Dried Hibiscus

Dried Raspberries

Lemons & Limes

Tabasco

Angostura Bitters

Bitter Truth Cucumber Bitters

Regans' Orange Bitters No. 6

& BEER...

IPA, Stout, Pilsner

NOTES

NOTES

NOTES

NOTES

Photo Credits:

Peter Clark: B&W Oli
Olimax: All colour portraits & Gros artwork
George Mulholland & Yam Montaña: Cocktails
Craig Hunt: Sepia Kilt, Eat Meat Edibles & Oli Selfies

Editor-in-Chief: Rick Sareen

THANK YOU

George Mulholland
Rick & Su Sareen
Kelly Brantner
Dorian Crook
Tony Cadman
Tamsen Hiles
Yam & Nina
Peter Clark
Jonas Linde
Craig Hunt
Rai & Katy
Nookie
Carlos
Farika
Julia Fossi
Anastasia
Rubén Pol
Family Hiles
Karin & Rafe
Dick Bradsell
Sophie Parkin
Kathy & Gass
Óscar Valero
Elin Svensson
Dani & Valeria
Tim Broadbent
Matthew Sanger
Lee & Dani Harris
Paul Vincent Lawford
Dave 'the Hat' McGowan
Shaun Pilgrem Vandersteen
Pepe, Jaume and everyone at Singlot
The French House & all who sail in her

Also by Olimax

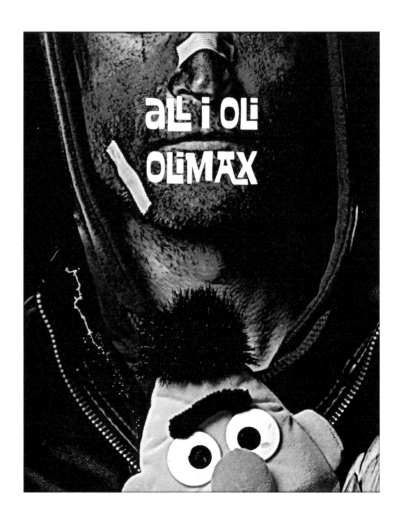

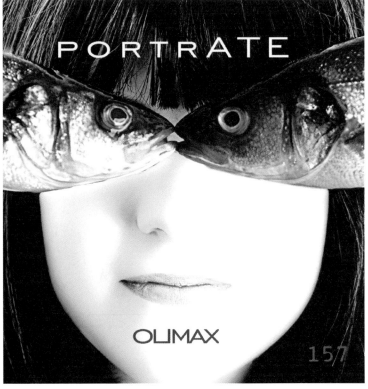

Printed in Poland
by Amazon Fulfillment
Poland Sp. z o.o., Wrocław
03 March 2023